Dragonflies of the
North Woods

Dragonflies
of the North Woods
By Kurt Mead

Kollath-Stensaas
PUBLISHING

Kollath-Stensaas Publishing
394 Lake Avenue South, Suite 406
Duluth, MN 55802
218. 727. 1731
kollath@cpinternet.com

DRAGONFLIES *of the* NORTH WOODS

Printed in Korea by Doosan Printing
10 9 8 7 6 5 4 3 2 1   First Edition

Editorial Director: Mark Sparky Stensaas
Graphic Designer: Rick Kollath

ISBN 0-9673793-6-9

Table of Contents

What is a Dragonfly? 1

Dragonfly Biology 101 5

Behavior of the "Winged Dragons" 9

Dragonfly Observation 12

How to Use this Field Guide 18

Species Accounts 22

Darners (Aeshnidae) 22

Aeshna (Blue Darners) 26
Anax (Green Darner) 46
Boyeria (Spotted Darners) 48
Nasiaeschna (Cyrano Darner) 52
Gomphaeschna (Pygmy Darners) 53
Epiaeschna (Swamp Darner) 54
Basiaeschna (Springtime Darner) 55

Clubtails (Gomphidae) 56

Hagenius (Dragonhunter) 58
Gomphus (Common Clubtails) 60
Stylurus (Hanging Clubtails) 74
Dromogomphus (Spinylegs) 78
Arigomphus (Pond Clubtails) 80
Stylogomphus (Least Clubtails) 82
Progomphus (Sanddragons) 83
Ophiogomphus (Snaketails) 84

Spiketails (Cordulegastridae) 92

Cordulegaster (Spiketails) 93

Cruisers (Macromiidae) 99

Didymops (Brown Cruisers) 100
Macromia (River Cruisers) 102

Emeralds (Corduliidae) 104

Cordulia (Common Emeralds) 106
Dorocordulia (Little Emeralds) 108
Williamsonia (Boghaunters) 109
Tetragoneuria (Baskettails) 110
Epicordulia (Prince Baskettail) 115
Somatochlora (Striped Emeralds) 116
Neurocordulia (Shadowdragons) 134

Skimmers (Libellulidae) 136

Libellula (King Skimmers) 138
Sympetrum (Meadowhawks) 150
Nannothemis (Elfin Skimmer) 164
Pachydiplax (Blue Dasher) 166
Erythemis (Pondhawks) 168
Pantala (Rainpool Gliders) 170
Leucorrhinia (Whitefaces) 172
Celithemis (Small Pennants) 182
Tramea (Saddlebag Gliders) 184

Common Damselflies 186

Glossary 188

Appendix A
Checklist of
North Woods Dragonflies 190

Appendix B
World Dragonfly Synonyms 193

Appendix C
Phenology Flight Chart 194

Appendix D & E
Dragonfly Groups & Websites
Photo Credits 196

Appendix F
Titles of Interest 197

Appendix G
Binoculars for Dragonflying 198

Index 200

To Dr. Janet Rith-Najarian
who started the ball rolling and has
impacted so many Minnesotans with her
passion for dragonflies.

And to my daughters, Yarrow and Lily:
May you someday find a passion as rich
and rewarding as mine has been.

Acknowledgements

About ten years ago, I blurted out to my wife Betsey, "Someday I'm going to write a book." She smiled and nodded, actually believing that I someday would, but knowing that it was not going to be soon. Then, after harassing Sparky for a few years about getting someone to write a regional field guide to the dragonflies, he asked me if I had a few photos for a dragonfly guide. I said I did and that I would work on getting a few more. I called him some weeks later to ask some questions and to find out who was writing the book. He responded with, "Well you are, aren't you?" I told him, of course, that was fine. I hung up the phone and ran, terrified, to find Betsey. I have calmed down some since that moment, and I thank Sparky and Rick for giving me the opportunity to write this book.

My parents, Scott and Phyllis Mead, are to be credited with giving me the opportunity to run free as a child. We explored the natural world at home on the farm, on our many family vacations and during hunting and fishing trips. They have always been supportive and understanding.

To Dave Palmquist, Minnesota Department of Natural Resources naturalist at Whitewater State Park, thank you for sharing your excitement and passion for the natural world. The seed you planted continues to grow today.

Thanks go to John Salek, my high school biology teacher in Plainview, Minnesota for introducing me to taxonomy and an appreciation for the diversity of life.

Jay Shaw and Aaron Henne have kept me in computers, and assorted hardware and software, while I crashed hard drives and burned up motherboards on a regular basis.

My brother-in-law, Robert Mancieri, helped me get my photography skills up to the late twentieth century (where I intend to stay).

Jocelyn Pihlaja, my favorite "cuz'," thoroughly reviewed and edited much of my rough manuscript.

Bob DuBois of the Wisconsin DNR enthusiastically reviewed much of my manuscript, provided good council and offered many nuggets of information that are sprinkled throughout this guide. He also gave us access to his extensive dragonfly collection for use in illustration.

Thanks to Colin Jones of the Ontario Ministry of Natural Resources and Algonquin Provincial Park who provided me with Ontario's North Woods dragonfly list which was very helpful in establishing our check-list for this book.

The staff at Wolf Ridge Environmental Learning Center in Finland, Minnesota has graciously put up with my obsession and on occasion provided me with a dozen eager teenagers with nets. Thank you.

A standing ovation for my wife, Betsey, for encouraging me in my quest to be an environmental educator and for mentoring me as a teacher. I could not have done it without you. Thank you also for tolerating my quirky ways and the piles of papers, books, diskettes, dead insects and candy wrappers that litter our home office.

Thanks to all in the World Dragonfly Association who have taken a "teneral" dragonfly enthusiast and welcomed him into their fold.

Finally, I thank Dr. Janet Rith-Najarian for opening the door to the world of dragonflies, for me and for many others in Minnesota and beyond. I stumbled into Janet at Wolf Ridge. She was sitting cross-legged on the canoe landing examining the emerging dragonflies that surrounded her. I was hooked. She patiently mentored and encouraged me and helped me to get the wind under my wings.

Writing *Dragonflies of the North Woods* has been an exciting and rewarding project for me. I hope you enjoy it.

To everyone: Thanks!

Kurt Mead

June 1, 2003

Kollath-Stensaas Publishers wish to thank Kurt for his full involvement in this major undertaking. His enthusiasm for dragonflies is contagious.

Thanks to Catherine Long for proofreading the manuscript and finding those big and little mistakes that had eluded us. And to Blair Nikula and Bob DuBois for keeping all our Odonata facts in check.

Susan Gustafson also gave us technical help that no one else could have given.

We used many of Kurt's splendid photographs and some of our own, and filled in the gaps with images from Blair Nikula, Robbye Johnson, John Webber, Sid Dunkle and Larry West—all fine naturalists in their own right.

The Publishers: Mark Sparky Stensaas, Rick Kollath

June 10, 2003

Parts of the Dragonfly

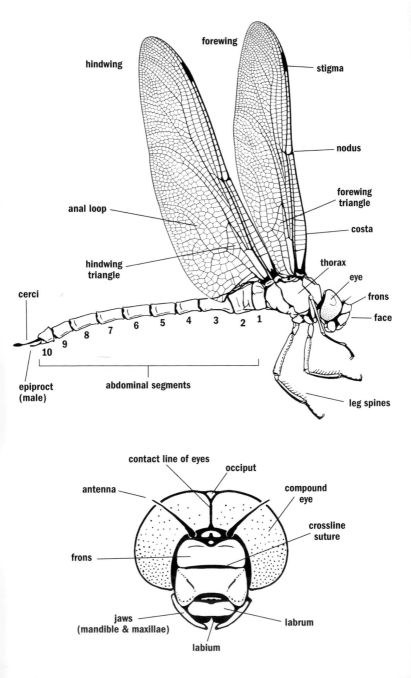

What is a Dragonfly?

"What's the use of their having names," the Gnat said, "if they won't answer to them?"

"No use to them," said Alice; "but it's useful to the people that name them I suppose."

—Lewis Carrol

When we talk about insects in general terms, we use commonly accepted names for large groups such as the beetles, the wasps, the ants and the butterflies and moths. All of these common names indicate the scientific order in which these bugs have been placed. The beetles are in the order Coleoptera. The butterflies and moths are in the order Lepidoptera. Dragonflies and damselflies are in the order **Odonata**.

A quick translation of the word odonata is "toothed ones," a reference to the awesome, toothy lower lip, or labium, which is used to capture and hold prey while their mandibles do the eating. "Odonata" was coined by the entomologist Fabricius in 1793.

Anisoptera, the suborder of the dragonflies, means "different wings" as their hindwings are distinctly larger and differently shaped than their forewings. The damselflies are in the suborder **Zygoptera**, which means "same wings," as their forewings and hindwings are about the same size and shape.

Dragonflies	**Damselflies**
Eyes in contact with each other *(except clubtails)*	Eyes always separate
Ovipositor non-functional *(except in some darners)*	Ovipositor present and functional
Stout build	Slight build
Strong, sustained flight	Weak, fluttery flight
Wings held flat when perched	Wings held over back *(except spreadwings)*

Dragonfly Parts

Like all insects, the dragonfly is made up of three main body parts: head, thorax and abdomen. The **head** is a tough, rounded capsule, hollowed out at the back to allow efficient attachment of the neck and to increase head mobility. The **mouth** is a complex hodgepodge of structures that you would not want to encounter in a dark alley. The upper lip, or **labrum**, is often considered part of the face. The lower lip, the **labium** (sometimes called the chin), is made up of three lobes. The labrum and labium function together to capture and secure prey while the jaws do the chewing. The **jaws**, which work from side to side, are made up of one pair of upper **mandibles** and two pairs of lower **maxillae**. These jaws, a series of incurved meat hooks, are worth a close inspection and should be approached with caution in larger species. A Dragonhunter and a large darner have both drawn blood from the thin skin between my fingers as I removed the beasts from my net. I hold no grudges; I suppose I had it coming.

The **face** is a conglomeration of plates separated by seams called **sutures**. The sutures are often darkened into stripes. The upper half of the face is the **frons**, and the upper surface of the frons is a shelf-like protuberance on which various diagnostic markings may be found. The **compound eye** is composed of nearly 30,000 lenses, which work in

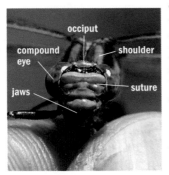

consort to provide a rich visual image to the dragonfly. They are sight-based creatures who, with a quick turn of the head, are able to scan 360 degrees as well as above and below. Their vision probably allows them to discern individual wing beats, which to us would appear as a blur. They can see ultraviolet and polarized light. Many species also see well in dim light.

Their two short bristly **antennae** are thought to function as windsocks or anemometers, measuring wind direction and speed, thereby giving them a

Most dragonflies have eyes that contact each other. Clubtails (as pictured above) are the exception.

method with which to assess their flight. By the way, dragonflies have no sense of hearing, cannot smell and are unable to vocalize.

The **thorax** is the center for locomotion. It is a muscular power-house, controlling head, wing and leg movements. Dragonflies are unusual in their wing movements. Most insects' wings are attached to plates of the chitonous exoskeleton that are, in turn, attached to muscles that move the plates that move the wings. Dragonfly wings, on the other hand, are directly connected to large muscles within the thorax. The interior of the **thoracic exoskeleton** is massively braced and strengthened to withstand the pressures of these large flight muscles. This bracing can be seen through the exoskeletons of lightly-pigmented individuals such as the Wandering Glider, the Four-spotted Skimmer and the Common Green Darner.

Thoracic stripes are present in many species. In order to easily communicate the positions of these stripes, the thorax can be separated into three sections: top, shoulder and sides. The **top stripes** of the thorax will be found in the region between the head and the wings and are best viewed from the front of the dragonfly. The **side stripes** of the thorax are found below the hindwing attachment point and back toward the abdomen. The **shoulder stripes** are found below the forewing attachment point, in between the top stripes and the side stripes.

Legs are used for perching and for capturing prey. Many species have **spines** on the legs that form a type of basket in which prey is caught. Check out the large spines on the Black-shouldered Spinyleg (page 78).

The anatomy of **wings** and their venation can be very complicated, and one could make a life's work of just studying them. Most dragonflies can be identified to the level of genus and many to the level of species by just knowing the wing venation. The **veins** in the wings of dragonflies start as flattened tubes in the compact, tightly folded wings hidden inside the skin of the aquatic nymph. During transformation to adulthood, the veins fill with **hemolymph**, or insect blood, causing the wings to unfurl. Most of the hemolymph is drawn

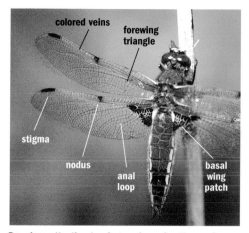

Pay close attention to wing marks and patterns when out dragonflying. They often help in identification.

back into the body after the wings have been fully expanded. The empty tubes and the membranes dry, leaving crisp, tough wings.

The most obvious feature of a clear, unpatterned wing is the **stigma**, located on the leading edge of each wing out towards the wingtips. It is thought that the stigma may be used for signaling mates or rivals and may also act as a tiny weight that dampens wing vibrations. The **nodus**, located at the shallow notch midway down the leading edge of each wing, is an intersection of several large veins and is a point of both strength and flexibility. Because of the structure of the venation around the nodus, the wing is allowed to bend downward (during an upward stroke of the wing) but not upward (during a downward stroke of the wing), resulting in a powerful flight stroke without losing much energy on the return stroke. The **wing triangles** are located about twenty percent of the way from the wing base toward the tip. The relative size and orientation of these triangles on a dragonfly's wings can be a clue as to the dragonfly's family. Originating from an inner, rear corner of the hindwing triangle, the **anal loop** reaches down into the expanded base of the hindwing. The degree to which the anal loop is present varies from one family to the next.

The **abdomen** always has ten **segments**. Segments 1 and 2 appear to be integrated into the thorax and are sometimes difficult to tell from the thorax. To find a particular segment, it is usually best to start with

club

The widened end of the abdomen is called a "club." The Skillet Clubtail has a very large club.

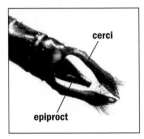

cerci

epiproct

Male claspers are comprised of the lower epiproct and the upper cerci. They are used to hold the female's head during mating.

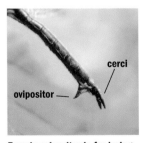

cerci

ovipositor

Female ovipositor is for laying eggs. This emerald's is spout-like and perpendicular.

segment 10, far out at the tip, and count backwards. Because of its segmented nature, the abdomen is very flexible and is able to arch up or down (but not side to side). Learn to count abdomen segments as many of our descriptions are based on them.

The male testes are located in segment 9. Due to the unique nature of dragonfly copulation, the male must transfer sperm to his secondary genitalia, called the **hamulus**, located in the underside of the second and third segments. The hamulus is a complicated set of "surgical tools" that the male uses for removing the reproductive "investment" made by other males during previous matings. Other parts of the hamulus are then used by the male to fertilize the female with his own sperm. The terminal abdominal appendages of the male are called **claspers**. The claspers are formed by a pair of upper appendages, called **cerci**, and a single lower appendage, an **epiproct**. In some species, the males possess **auricles** on the sides of segment 2 whose function is to help direct the female's genitalia to a proper fit with the male's secondary genitalia during copulation.

The female terminal appendages consist of a pair of **cerci**, which have little or no function. In some species, namely the Shadow Darner, they are very brittle and tend to break off. Underneath segment 8 there is either an **ovipositor** or a **subgenital plate**, depending upon the species. Both structures are for laying eggs and extend over segment 9 and possibly beyond.

The male abdomen is often narrower ("**waisted**") at segment 3, whereas the female abdomen is almost always more robust.

Dragonfly Biology 101

Mating

In most species, male dragonflies are fiercely competitive over preferred breeding and mating sites. Only the dominant males will get an opportunity to mate; others will be driven away. Competitions between males include sparring, flight contests and **threat displays** of bright colors on the abdomen or wings. Female dragonflies are not sexually competitive, but, like many males, they will compete with other dragonflies for the best feeding grounds.

Prior to the selection of a willing female, the male will transfer sperm from his testes located on the underside of abdominal segment 9 to his hamulus located on the underside of segments 2 and 3. This is accomplished by simply arching the abdomen until the undersides of the appropriate segments make contact. Mating is normally initiated by the male who, with the grace of a professional wrestler, uses his legs to grasp the female by her head and thorax. Curving his abdomen forward, he uses his two cerci and the lower

A mating pair of Variable Darners in the "wheel position." The male (the blue one) grasps the yellow-form female behind her head with his claspers as he transfers his sperm packet to her.

epiproct as a clamp and clasps the female by the back of the head. They are now "**in tandem**." Mating is accomplished by the male arching his abdomen downward while the female arches her abdomen toward the male's hamulus. Once connected, the pair is in the **wheel position** or "**in copula**." Still connected, the pair will usually fly up to the safety of treetops to mate, although some species do copulate in mid flight. The male commences a purging of the female's genital opening. He uses the hamulus to remove, squash or push out of the way any sperm that the female may still be carrying from prior matings with other males. This process ensures his genetic investment in the clutch of eggs that the female will soon lay. The time needed to complete fertilization ranges from 15 seconds to well over an hour.

Guarding & Egg Laying

After the completion of copulation, the couple may split up, or they may stay together through **oviposition,** i.e. **egg laying**. In some species, the male guards the female from the competition of other rivals and possibly even from predators. In other species the female is left alone to lay her eggs. **Guarding** may take several forms. The most basic form is **contact guarding**, where the male stays attached to the female for the entire egg-laying process. **Hover guarding** is another strategy in which

the male hovers above or perches near the female as she is laying eggs. From this vantage point he can attack and chase away from his territory any competing suitors as well as mate with any other females that enter his territory. A hover-guarding male may attempt to protect several of "his" egg-laying females at a time.

Metamorphosis of the aquatic larvae to the terrestrial adult dragonfly takes place on land. After clamping on to a log, grass stem, dock, etc. the larval case splits open and the thorax and head emerge.

There is also a rare type of guarding known as **karate guarding** where the protective male actually clasps a trespassing male, much as he would grab a prospective mate, and holds him until the guarded female has laid her eggs.

After a wriggling struggle, the abdomen is finally pulled free, wings still crumpled over its back.

There are many different oviposition, or egg-laying, strategies employed by dragonflies. Many female darners use their lance-like ovipositors to insert eggs into plant stems, sphagnum moss, rotting wood or wet soil. But most species of dragonflies possess non-functional ovipositors. Eggs must be washed off into water during flight as the female dips the tip of her abdomen into the lake, pond, river or stream. Other dragonflies have special flanges that flank the genital opening, allowing them to strike the surface of the water, purposefully splashing eggs into the water. Some females plunge the entire tip of their abdomen into mud or silt to deposit eggs. Others simply sprinkle eggs over a suitable habitat.

Among the many parasites that may infest dragonflies, by far the most common is the water mite (*Hydracarina* species). The larval mites attach themselves to larval dragonflies and feed off of their host's body fluids. Very young nymphs and unhatched eggs may actually be killed by water mite larvae, whereas larger dragonfly larvae are able to survive such an onslaught and may host a myriad of water mites. Look also for the tiny red critters on the legs and thorax of adult dragonflies.

Life as an Aquatic Larva

Many people are astounded to hear that the stately and colorful dragonfly spends the majority of its life as a drab, creepy-looking underwater larva. Unlike butterflies or mosquitoes, which undergo a complete, four-stage metamorphosis, dragonflies undergo three stages of development known as **incomplete metamorphosis**. There is no pupal stage in the life of a dragonfly. Incomplete metamorphosis consists of the egg, the larva (**nymph**) and the adult.

After the egg hatches, the free-crawling aquatic **larva** molts once and then starts hunting voraciously. As the larva grows, it will molt numerous times. Most dragonfly larvae mature to adulthood in one to three years. There are exceptions. The migratory Wandering Glider will take as few as four weeks to complete its development from egg to adult, whereas there are Asian species that take as long as 8 years to mature to adulthood. Some species known from the far North take longer to mature than the same species in more southerly environs. Water temperature and the length of the growing season are variables that help determine the length of maturation.

A day or two prior to emergence from the aquatic to the aerial form, the larva goes into a state of **diapause**, or rest, while the final changes are made inside the larval exoskeleton. They may some-

Hemolymph (insect blood) is pumped through the wing veins until fully expanded. After about an hour of rest, they fly off, masters of the air!

times rest with a part of their head above water to facilitate the transition to breathing air.

Emergence

Emergence, the transition from aquatic larva to adult dragonfly, usually takes place very early in the morning while clinging to a vertical or diagonal surface such as a plant stem, rock face, tree trunk, dock or bridge abutment, although many clubtails emerge from a horizontal position. When in position, the larva hooks its claws into the perch.

After a short period of rest, the skin at the back of the head cracks open, and the thorax emerges from the larval skin. The split enlarges down the back, and the head, compressed wings, legs and part of the abdomen are forced out. The dragonfly rests again, arched backwards and hanging from its unreleased abdomen. During this time, the legs harden. Grabbing its shedding larval case with its "new" legs, the dragonfly pulls its abdomen free. The abdomen extends, and the wings unfurl as they fill with hemolymph (blood). After a short while, the hemolymph is drawn back into the body, and then the juvenile, or **teneral dragonfly,** rests, letting the wings dry for

A newly emerged Common Green Darner (teneral) leaves behind its larval shell (exuviae).

about an hour before the first flight is attempted. The discarded **exuviae**—the empty larval shell— will remain "perched" until wind, rain or a curious naturalist removes it. By the time a dragonfly makes its first flight, it is at full, adult size. Little dragonflies are not babies; they are full grown adults. No more molting will take place after they leave their larval case behind.

Transformation is a very vulnerable time for the dragonfly. As much as 90 percent mortality has been observed in a population due to bird predation. Many dragonflies are ready to fly soon after sunrise, a potentially successful strategy used to avoid being eaten by the "early bird." Spiders and ants eat their fair share of young dragonflies, as well.

Behavior of the "Winged Dragons"

Fearsome Predators

During all stages of their lives, dragonflies are fearsome and efficient hunters. If dragonfly larvae were eight to sixteen inches long, as they probably were 300 million years ago, we would dare not swim in fresh water for fear of being attacked. Any moving, living thing could be prey for dragonfly larvae, including other dragonfly larvae, daphnia, mosquito larvae, tadpoles and even small fish. (Several of my daughter's goldfish fell prey to my good intentions when I brought home a large Common Green Darner larva. At the time, she didn't appreciate the scientific aspects of the experience at all.) Aquatic larvae are very visual; any nearby movement is noticed. Their antennae are very sensitive and are used as tactile sensors, picking up even slight movement. Prey is secured primarily through the use of the powerful, extendable lower lip (labium) that is equipped with "teeth." In as little as $1/100$ of a second, the labium can be extended out to $1/3$ the length of its body, snagging the victim with the teeth and delivering it to the waiting jaws underneath.

Some dragonfly larvae, such as the darners, stalk their prey among the plants and detritus of their underwater jungle. These **"crawlers"** are able to see a moving target from a distance of several inches and will slowly pursue prey in a cat-like manner until within striking distance. Other larvae, such as the emeralds, skimmers and the long-legged cruisers, are **"sprawlers,"** blending into the bottom materials with camouflaging markings or by a build up of silt on body hairs. Sprawlers lay in wait with their antennae laid out on the muck or sand until suitable prey happens by. A third hunting style is demonstrated by the **"burrowers."** Most clubtails (with the exception of the Dragonhunter, a massive sprawler) and spiketails are burrowers who disappear below the

The aquatic larvae (nymphs) of dragonflies are ferocious predators. This Dragonhunter nymph (note the leaf-like body and long legs) patrols a sandy lake bottom in the Boundary Waters.

sand or silt, only their eyes and the tips of their abdomens are visible. They lunge at anything that comes within striking distance.

Despite their skill as predators, the larvae are also heavily preyed upon by fish, birds, predatory aquatic insects and other dragonfly nymphs. Larval gills are located inside their abdomen and water must be pulled in through the rectum and expelled for them to breathe. To avoid predators they accelerate this process and effectively become "jet propelled."

Adults are also fearsome predators that have even been known to take down a hummingbird. Their hunting prowess is due in no small part to large eyes, resilient and maneuverable wings, spiky legs that form a snagging net and a powerful, muscular thorax serving both the wings and the legs. Adult dragonflies capture exclusively live prey and almost always while they are on the wing. Flying insects are located visually and smaller prey is caught directly by the mouth. Larger insects are snared in a basket that the dragonfly forms with its legs, transferring the food to its mouth after it has been secured. Prey is either eaten on the wing or from a perch. The hard parts of beetles and wings of butterflies, moths, damselflies and other larger insects are discarded and may be found below a favored perch by the observant naturalist. If you can approach close enough to a chewing dragonfly you will be able to hear them "crunch, crunch" on the exoskeleton of their "McBug" sandwich.

Temperature Control

Because warmth is needed for activity and an efficient metabolism, most dragonflies disappear to protected perches on cool days or when the sun disappears behind a cloud. Despite the fact that insects are "cold blooded," many dragonflies maintain an internal temperature as high as 110 degrees F. This is accomplished by the burning of calories

This Blue Dasher is in the "obelisk position." Orienting its abdomen towards the sun reduces its exposure to solar radiation and prevents overheating.

during physical exertion and by staying in the sun. A cold dragonfly preparing to get the day started will shiver its wings to create heat in its thorax until it has warmed itself enough to take flight. Some dragonflies, such as the Ebony Boghaunter, Stygian Shadowdragon and the blue darners have adapted to cooler weather as a method of allowing early- or late-season emergence or to take advantage of the plethora of insect life that becomes active at dusk. Some species will be seen flying well after sunset on moonlit evenings or under street lights.

In hot, sunny weather it is important that dragonflies don't overheat. Cooling strategies include becoming less active, moving into shade and changing their body position. The **obelisk position** orients the dragonfly's abdomen directly at the sun, thereby reducing the surface area exposed to solar heating. Some dragonflies also point their wings forward and down in order to reduce exposure to sunlight and, perhaps, to reflect light and heat away from their bodies.

Dragonflies drink by thrusting their bodies down onto the water's surface in a sequence of one to three splashdowns. Water is absorbed through the exoskeleton. Dew is also absorbed on cool mornings.

Migration

Certain species of dragonfly migrate, either en masse or individually. Dragonflies follow weather fronts, fleeing cold fronts in the fall on their way south and chasing warm fronts in the spring when moving north.

The best-known migrant is the Common Green Darner, who makes a one-way trip south in the fall and whose offspring makes the return one-way trip north the following spring. Another seasonal migrator is the Variegated Meadowhawk who may be seen in early spring returning from year-round haunts in Oklahoma or Texas. It is risky business though, as April snow and cold can strand and freeze thousands.

Frank Nicoletti, the head hawk-counter at Hawk Ridge in Duluth, has observed that the peak American Kestrel migration every fall coincides with the peak Common Green Darner migration down the North Shore of Lake Superior. He believes the kestrels rely on the large dragonflies as a food source during the trip south. While the kestrels tend to ignore the green darners at midday, concentrating rather on making miles, later in the afternoon they start feeding heavily on them.

On several occasions in the fall, I have observed flocks of migrating Common Nighthawks flying above swarms of Common Green Darners, both creatures feeding on masses of smaller flying insects. I have never once seen the nighthawks eat a darner, and both species tend to keep to their own space. The relationship appears to exist only due to the concentration of small insect prey.

Wintering

Unlike butterflies, there are no dragonflies that overwinter as adults in the North Woods. Most winter beneath the ice in the larval form in a state of diapause, which is a sort of suspended animation. Other species, such as some of the meadowhawks, lay their eggs along shorelines where the eggs will sit through the winter until high water in spring washes them into the lake.

Dragonfly Observation

Like birding and butterfly watching, proper identification involves close observation of minute details. Close-focusing binoculars are nearly essential in seeing colors and patterns in the field. Digital and film camera images also allow one to identify active subjects. But many important clues to separate closely related species need to be observed in the hand or with a hand lens magnifier. Because of the subtle differences, it is impossible to separate some species without catching them. So if you choose not to use a net, you need to adjust your identification expectations. Most dragonflies can be identified to the level of genus and some to the level of species by observing them at a distance.

Unlike birding, the best time for dragonfly observation usually occurs after a long, late breakfast, complete with an extra cup of coffee.

Early risers, though, may be rewarded with the opportunity to witness the shoreline transformation of larval dragonflies into adults. The emergence process is slow and magical and worth the occasional sunrise trip.

For the beginner, "dragonflying" may simply entail noting colors, wing patterns (or lack thereof), sizes, behaviors and habitat preferences of the different

All ages enjoy the hobby of "dragonflying." Learning to handle live insects is just one fascinating aspect.

odonates that whiz past. The next step is to start stalking dragonflies in their specific habitats with close-focusing binoculars, camera or net.

The basic traits that help in identifying dragonflies to family are listed in the header section for each family. Knowing the families well will provide a firm base from which to confidently plunge into the more-detailed aspects of dragonfly identification. It is best to start slowly. Don't start trying to identify to species all of the confusing meadowhawks (genus *Sympetrum*) or whitefaces (genus *Leucorrhinia*) on your first outing. That's a sure path to frustration.

Habitats and Seasons

Knowing a little about a species' habitat requirements and seasonal occurrence may help determine where and when to go to find a particular dragonfly. All animals have specific habitat needs and won't thrive, or even survive, if those needs are not met. In this guide, very specific habitat information has been provided for each species' preferred breeding sites, but generalizations can made about some groups of dragonflies. Remember though, during the maturation period, after transformation from larva to adult, a dragonfly usually flies afield, sometimes far from their preferred breeding and rearing habitats. When it comes time to reproduce, however, the dragonfly will return to the preferred habitat.

During spring and early summer many dragonfly enthusiasts focus on the rivers and swift streams of the North Woods, looking for the exciting clubtail species (Gomphidae). These riverine environments provide the highly oxygenated and unsilted waters that early-emerging clubtails demand.

Bogs, open swamps, marshes and smaller, muck-bottomed lakes in late spring are where the tiny whitefaces (genus *Leucorrhinia*) will be found, whereas later in the summer the same habitat may be swarming with little red and yellow meadowhawks (genus *Sympetrum*).

Many species in the Skimmer family (Libellulidae) are considered pond species and the larvae will be found in smaller, quiet bodies of water, as well as in sheltered portions of larger lakes. Skimmers tend to dominate the middle of the summer, though they may also be among the earliest and latest species present in the North Woods.

From July through September, the blue darners (genus *Aeshna*) may be seen along lakeshores and in open, wooded areas near water.

Find cool, small streams that flow through remote northern swamps or bogs in the middle of the summer and there will be striped emeralds (genus *Somatochlora*) flitting about.

Quiet bog pools are the preferred breeding grounds for many dragonfly species in the North. Courtship, mating and egg laying will take place here. Their larvae will develop on the pond's bottom, eating voraciously until it is time to emerge.

Phenological events happen every year, and one of these annual milestones is the arrival of the first dragonflies of the year. The Common Green Darner migrates north with the warm weather and, sometimes arrives before the ice is completely off of our northern lakes. This charismatic dragonfly will take its chances with late frosts and snows. Conversely, in the fall, their progeny will move south, en masse, with cool weather nipping at their epiprocts, to reach the relative safety of warmer southern waters. Just after the arrival of the migrant green darners in the spring, an explosion of baskettails (genus *Tetragoneuria*) may occur near boggy lakes, ponds and streams, the hordes filling any nearby clearing.

The author on a dragonflying foray near his home in northern Minnesota. Knowing when and where a species may show up increases your chances of success.

Keep good notes. Fill a notebook with dates, locations, photos and sketches. The information you gather will help you immeasurably, not only in field identification, but also in where and when to look for different species. Any small notebook will do in a pinch, but one with waterproof paper, such as the *Rite-in-the-Rain*-style notebooks, will not turn to pulp when (not if…when) it gets wet. Pencil works best, as ink may run when soaked. Notes should include date, time, location, current and recent weather conditions, a description of the habitat, primary vegetation and the names of your field companions. There is nothing more pleasant on a cold winter day than sitting next to the woodstove, cup of hot tea in hand, and poring over last summer's field notes, reminiscing about past outings and planning next year's strategies.

Binoculars

Close-focusing binoculars are the number one tool you need to enjoy dragonflying. Today, many full-size binoculars focus to less than ten feet. Avoid any binocular that does not focus this close; note that most compacts do not focus close! A full explanation of binocular features and a buyers guide with specs on more than 38 models are found in Appendix G.

Photography

Close-up, or macro, photography is a fine way to record your finds for future enjoyment and identification. The advantages of compact digital cameras are that many have built in close focusing, they fit in a pocket, you are able to immediately see your pictures and you can edit as you go. Film cameras and digital SLRs (ones you can change the lenses on) still have the edge in shooting free-flying, unchilled dragon-flies since they give you greater working distance between the subject and lens. Compact digitals force you to be within inches of the subject. Check the Titles of Interest (Appendix F) on page 197 for the excellent books by John Shaw and Larry West on close-up 35mm photography.

It is important when photographing dragonflies to get shots of the insect from several different angles: top of the thorax, face, side view of thoracic markings, abdomen, abdominal appendages and top view showing the wings. Granted, when working with a free-flying specimen it may not be possible to get all of these views, but if you can, you should.

Chillin'

Captured specimens can be chilled and posed for photography. Unlike other refrigerated-insect photos, dragonflies shot in this way do look quite normal (though the colors of some will temporarily fade). Simply cooling the dragonfly for ten minutes will slow them down enough to be photographed on your terms for about three minutes. A small "6-pack" cooler equipped with ice or frozen gel-packs will work as a chiller in the field. Slip the live dragonfly into an envelope and pop it into the cooler tray (don't put it directly on the ice). You can lengthen the amount of time before your chilled dragonfly flies away by feeding it a live mosquito or a fly. Care should be taken to position the insect in a realistic pose in a realistic environment. This does not harm the dragonfly, but they can get slightly dehydrated, so I recommend rehydrating them by quickly dipping them into water before releasing.

Some dragonflies can only be positively identified when in the hand.

Scanners

Stunningly detailed digital images may be acquired using a flatbed scanner on your home computer. Cut a 6 x 6-inch square out of the middle of a thick computer mouse pad and lay the "frame" on the scanner glass. The opening in the pad will allow you to position the chilled dragonfly on the glass, under the closed lid, without crushing the insect. There are detailed instructions at various sites on the Internet.

Dragonfly Nets & Netting

Capturing dragonflies can be a challenge. My extended family treats my netting of dragonflies as a spectator sport. One cannot be timid or slow with a net when pursuing the "winged dragons," and one should expect to miss…often. When possible, dragonflies should be approached from below and behind, as this is their blind spot. Stalk perched dragonflies very slowly and deliberately. Many insects, including dragonflies, have trouble sensing a large object that is moving slowly towards them. The net bag should be held back against the handle to reduce its profile. As soon as a dragonfly is netted, the bag of the net should be flopped over, with a quick flip of the wrist, to trap the dragonfly down in the bottom. Reach carefully down through the folds of

the net and, using your index and middle fingers, gently fold all four wings over its back and carefully remove it from the net. Some of the largest dragonflies are able to nip your fingers, so be careful.

One of the most common nets has a deep net-bag with an 18-inch opening and an extendable handle that ranges in length from two feet

Only serious students of dragonflies should attempt to net and handle them. Improper handling of a live dragonfly can hurt or kill it.

to at least six feet. I prefer a collapsible net with one- or two-foot long aluminum handle sections (see BioQuip info on next page). This setup will fit easily in a daypack and is sturdy enough to endure some abuse. Many people prefer to make their own nets. A popular style of homemade net is made from a sturdy fish-landing net with the original netting replaced with mosquito netting. A homemade net can be made by bending a very sturdy wire loop, large enough to accommodate a net bag, and attaching the ends of the wire to a wooden dowel or lightweight pipe. Net bags can be made from mosquito or no-see-um netting, or they may be inexpensively purchased from BioQuip.

Hand Capturing

I learned this technique from European odonatologists who temporarily capture specimens for closer study. It only works on blue darners (genus *Aeshna*) perched vertically on tree trunks. From a distance of five to ten yards, slowly approach the dragonfly from behind. With arm extended, draw slow, broad circles in front of you with your fingertip. As you approach, gradually spiral your arm down, in smaller and smaller circles, to the point where the dragonfly is close enough to gently trap against the tree trunk or grab with your fingers. Another method is to gently grab a perched dragonfly that has been stilled by the cold, such as in early morning and during fall cold snaps.

Collecting Conundrum

The question of whether to collect or not to collect dragonfly specimens is a subject that elicits strong opinions and emotions. All insect enthusiasts must make up their own mind as to whether they will have a bug collection or not. The World Dragonfly Association and the Dragonfly Society of the Americas both have Responsible Collecting Guidelines that should be read by anyone considering a collection of dragonflies.

Capturing darners by hand is a skill that takes technique, patience and practice.

Collecting and preserving techniques are beyond the scope of this book, but instructions are available on their websites (see Appendix D).

A Lifetime Hobby

No matter how you approach the hobby of dragonflying, it is sure to become an enjoyable and educational lifetime endeavor.

Equipment Sources

BioQuip Products: A wide selection of aerial nets (including the popular collapsible net), aquatic nets, Odonata envelopes, field guides, scopes and other entomological equipment.
310. 324. 0620
www.bioquip.com

Acorn Naturalists: A great source for aerial nets, aquatic nets, books, and other naturalist and teaching resources.
800. 422. 8886
www.acornnaturalists.com

International Odonatological Research Institute: Best source for collecting envelopes. Also field guides and other books.
http://www.afn.org/~iori/

How to use this Field Guide

Dragonflies of the North Woods is designed to make field identification easier for you, the reader. Through the use of color photos, arrows pointing to field marks, size scales, phenograms and habitats, we have made a handy, compact and easy to use guide. Also, by limiting the dragonflies to those found in one geographic area, we have eliminated the need to wade through several hundred species, many of which would never be found here. Included is every regularly occurring dragonfly in the North Woods of the Western Great Lakes.

For the purposes of this book we will define the North Woods as the area underlain by the granite of the Canadian Shield. This would encompass northeast Minnesota, northern Wisconsin, the Upper Peninsula of Michigan, parts of Ontario, Quebec and New England. This book focuses on Minnesota, Wisconsin, Michigan and northwest Ontario. But remember, not all species are found in any single area. Habitat preferences tend to spread species out. The North Woods is a mosaic of different dragonfly habitats from lakes, ponds and marshes to rivers, streams and bog pools.

Order

Dragonflies are organized by families and then broken down further into genera. Family name is listed at the bottom of the left page of each species spread while the genus is listed on the bottom of the right page. We placed closely related species next to each other. With experience in the field using this guide, you will gradually learn to identify dragonflies to family.

Dragonfly Names

Like other organisms, dragonflies are given both common and scientific names. The common names are the English names most amateur naturalists use, while the scientific or Latin names tend to be the spoken word of odonatologists. We capitalize species names but use lower case for groups (e.g. <u>B</u>lue <u>D</u>ashers are actually a type of <u>s</u>kimmer).

Photos

We chose to use photos of free-flying dragonflies in their natural habitat. Some are chilled specimens that resumed their normal activities minutes after the photo was taken. Images were acquired from seven different photographers. (Photo credits are listed on page 196.) We attempted to use photos that illustrated the best field marks. Sexual dimorphism (different coloration in males and females) is the norm for some species; we label the photos as male or female in these cases.

Abundance

A blue circle on each photo shows the relative abundance of each species: C=common, FC=fairly common, U=unusual, R=rare and VR=very rare. Of course, even a "rare" species may be locally common if you happen to be in their preferred habitat at the right time.

Fieldmark Arrows

Arrows point to diagnostic features in the photos that are referenced in the description text and marked with an arrow symbol (↑). These are characteristics that you should look for while in the field. Jotting down notes on size, color, thoracic stripes, abdomen markings and wing features will help you identify the dragonfly when you have a chance to consult this book.

Size Scale

Size is relative and often hard to judge in the field. Use the size-bars at the top of each species' main photo. The black bar indicates the actual body length of that species.

Black size-bar shows actual body length for the species.

The red phenogram indicates when you are most likely to see that dragonfly on the wing.

Blue buttons estimate the relative abundance of that species.

Photos on the right side of the spread may show a different angle, females and/or juveniles.

Nature Notes **are natural history tidbits about that species.**

Habitats where courtship, mating, egg laying and larval development take place.

Family name is listed on the lower left hand page and genus is found on the right page.

Phenograms

What is a phenogram? All dragonflies live out their lives according to seasonal timing that is characteristic and consistent for that species. Our phenogram highlights in red the time when that species is active as a flying adult. In other words, look for that dragonfly during the highlighted weeks/months. This can also help narrow down your identification search. Let's say you see a darner in mid May with blue abdominal spots. By field characteristics you think it could have been either a Black-tipped Darner or a Springtime Darner. Noting the phenograms for each, you conclude that it most likely was a Springtime Darner since Black-tipped Darners do not usually emerge until July.

Habitat

Preferred habitat is found beneath the phenogram. Remember, this is where courtship, mating and egg laying takes place, and the larva develops and emerges. Your best bet to find the species will probably be near such habitat—but not exclusively. Dragonflies can range widely over many different habitats.

Nature Notes

Nature Notes are fascinating bits of natural history that bring one a more complete understanding of that species. Unique behavior, population trends, migration, naming history and larval characteristics are just some of the topics touched on.

Species Text

Description covers the best distinguishing characteristics first—whether it is the abdomen markings, thoracic pattern, wing spots, veins, leg color or facial marks. If males and females are different (sexual dimorphism) then these differences are described. Measurements given are the average body length. If there is great variation in adults, a range of sizes is given.

Some of these differences can only be seen in the hand. We have tried not to delve too deeply into the realm of wing venation, claspers and ovipositors, fascinating and useful though they may be, unless it is absolutely necessary for positive identification.

Under **Similar Species**, other dragonflies that could be confused with that species are described and differences highlighted.

Flight Characteristics speaks to the unique way that dragonflies fly. Some hover, some have an undulating flight and some fly straight and fast. Only species that have a distinct flight are covered.

Hunting Technique describes the way the adults go about catching insect prey. Once again, this is only described when it is unique.

Mating & Egg Laying covers territoriality in males, mating positions, courtship, male guarding, egg laying technique and larval development.

Common Damselflies

We do not cover damselflies in this book, but we do include a two-page spread of the most common types you might see in the field. Damselfly identification is a tricky affair and few good references exist.

Glossary

Kurt has not used much technical jargon in the text, but check out the glossary for easy-to-understand meanings of some tricky terms.

North Woods Dragonfly Checklist

In Appendix A, you will find a checklist of all 100-plus species regularly found in the North Woods of Minnesota, Wisconsin, Michigan and northwest Ontario. Check off the ones you see in your travels afield.

World Dragonfly Synonyms

Myth and mystery have followed the dragonfly down through time. Check out Appendix B for the fascinating names that different cultures around the globe have given to odonates.

Phenology Flight Chart

An extremely useful Phenology Flight Chart is shown in Appendix C. This chart illustrates the flight times for some common dragonflies, starting with the earliest and continuing through to the late-season flyers. At a glance one can easily see which species would be likely during that time period. This is meant as a rough guide since seasonal variations from year to year, especially in early spring, can change emergence times. Add your own notes and dates to this chart to make it uniquely yours.

Dragonfly Groups & Websites

Dragonfly organizations are a great way to connect with like-minded folks. The websites listed are a great place to start. Appendix D.

Titles of Interest

This list of recommended reading and resources includes our favorite titles for delving deeper into the fascinating world of the "winged dragons." Also listed are books on close-up nature photography. Appendix F.

Binoculars for Dragonflying

Recommended binoculars are those that focus close and are of good quality. Check out Appendix G if you are in the market for new "glass."

Enjoy *Dragonflies of the North Woods.* Take it in the field. Cram it in your pack. Use it. But most importantly, have fun getting to know our fascinating northern dragonflies.

Darners
Family Aeshnidae

The darners are a large-bodied bunch, most being over 2½ inches long. They have slender abdomens and robust thoraxes. Huge eyes meet along a very long margin across the top of the head giving them a helmeted look. The hindwing and forewing triangles are equal in size.

The female has an ovipositor that is similar to that found on damselflies. Whereas most dragonflies scatter, dip or plunge their eggs into mud or water, female darners use their ovipositor like a stylet, piercing plant stems and inserting their eggs one at a time into the resulting hole. They do this without a male escort (except the Common Green Darner who oviposits while in tandem). Not to scare you, but I have read of rare, isolated reports of darners attempting to lay eggs into human skin. One scientist carefully observed eggs being injected into each cut in his skin. Perhaps this phenomenon is the source of some old European names such as "eye sticker," "horse stinger" and "devil's darning-needle."

Darners are voracious and formidable predators, preying upon insects both large and small. I once observed a large darner capture and eat a meadowhawk that I had just released from my net. They also devour damselflies. Although they will "graze" throughout the day, darners are fond of eating late, flying through dusk, becoming ghosts flitting about in the twilight.

The long, cylindrical aquatic larvae are are crawlers who stalk their prey amongst the plant litter and debris of the pond or stream bottom.

Most darners perch vertically on surfaces such as tree trunks, bush branches and grass stalks, but a few, such as the Zigzag Darner, are ground perchers.

We find 19 species of darners in the North Woods, 39 species in North America and about 500 species worldwide.

The Blue Darners — Genus *Aeshna*

Members of the genus *Aeshna* are often referred to as "blue darners" or "mosaic darners." They are large dragonflies with blue markings …except when the markings are green…and sometimes they are yellow …oh, and quite often they will have gradations of all three colors. Amazingly, all of this variability may occur within a single species!

All blue darners have two thoracic side stripes below the wings and two stripes on the front of the thorax, between the head and where the wings attach. Two rows of spots run down the length of the abdomen (the resulting patterns are the origin for the name "mosaic" darner). They have a black T-spot on top of the frons, just in front of where the eyes meet. The face is pale in color.

The male's abdominal appendages, or claspers, are used for holding the female behind the head during mating. There are two clasper types: wedge and paddle (see illustrations on this page). Paddle-type claspers are slightly upcurved at the ends (in profile) and are shaped like paddles from above. Wedge-type claspers terminate with a down-pointing tooth (in profile) and are more square off when viewed from above.

Observing blue darners at the edge of a pond you may note almost no females. Males regularly patrol their territories, but, unless the female is ready to mate and lay eggs, she keeps to the shelter of the forest. Entering a male's shoreline territory may lead to her being viciously grabbed by him or even by a group of males.

Several blue darner species possess impressive lance-like ovipositors that pierce plant stems to lay eggs.

Blue (Mosaic) Darners (Genus *Aeshna*)

24 Thorax Comparison Chart
26 Canada Darner
28 Green-striped Darner
30 Lake Darner
32 Black-tipped Darner
34 Shadow Darner
36 Lance-tipped Darner
38 Mottled Darner
39 Sedge Darner
40 Variable Darner
42 Subarctic Darner
44 Zigzag Darner

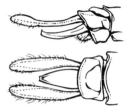

Paddle-type Claspers

Green Darners (Genus *Anax*)

46 Common Green Darner

Spotted Darners (Genus *Boyeria*)

48 Ocellated Darner
50 Fawn Darner

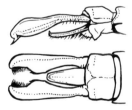

Wedge-type Claspers

Cyrano Darners (Genus *Nasiaeschna*)

52 Cyrano Darner

Pygmy Darners (Genus *Gomphaeschna*)

53 Harlequin Darner

Swamp Darners (Genus *Epiaeschna*)

54 Swamp Darner

Springtime Darners (Genus *Basiaeschna*)

55 Springtime Darner

"Blue Darner" Thorax Comparisons

All *Aeshna* species (the blue darners) have two side stripes on their thorax. Shape, color and width of these stripes can take one a long ways toward a positive identification. Refer to the species accounts for more field marks to look for when observing the blue darners.

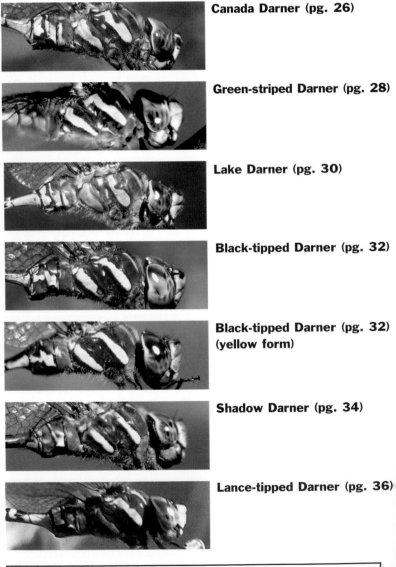

Canada Darner (pg. 26)

Green-striped Darner (pg. 28)

Lake Darner (pg. 30)

Black-tipped Darner (pg. 32)

Black-tipped Darner (pg. 32) (yellow form)

Shadow Darner (pg. 34)

Lance-tipped Darner (pg. 36)

Mottled Darner (pg. 38)

Sedge Darner (pg. 26)

Variable Darner (pg. 40)
(striped form)

Variable Darner (pg. 40)
(interrupted form)

Variable Darner (pg. 40)
(spotted form)

Subarctic Darner (pg. 42)

Zigzag Darner (pg. 44)

Canada Darner *Aeshna canadensis* (male)

| MAY | JUNE | JULY | AUG | SEPT | OCT | NOV |

Slow streams and lakes with boggy or marshy edges. Beaver ponds. Especially fond of waters with vegetated shallows and floating wood near mixed coniferous and deciduous trees.

Nature Notes:

The Canada is probably the most common of the blue darners (Genus *Aeshna*) throughout our range. I have found them so abundant, at times, that they can be a pest when I am trying to find other species.

Description: Adults average 2.8 inches long.

Adults: The front thoracic side stripe is deeply notched at a 90-degree angle ↑ and has a rearward extension off the top. The rear thoracic side stripe is not notched. Male stripes are often green below and blue above but can be all green or all blue; female has green thoracic side stripes. Her abdomen has green top spots with blue side spots. Green-form female has all green markings with wings tinted brown. Blue-form female resembles the male and is uncommon. No heavy black line across the face. Male claspers are of the paddle type.

Female green-form Canada Darners and female Green-striped Darners are not easy to tell apart.

Similar Species: The Lake Darner is larger than the Canada, has a black crossline on the face and its rear thoracic stripe is constricted in the middle. (See the discussion of female Green-striped vs. Canada on page 29.)

Hunting Technique: Fly almost constantly, eating in flight, until nightfall, flitting ghost-like in the cool of evening. Difficult to see without sunlight glinting off their wings, as they erratically turn and twist. They work stream edges and lakeshores systematically, missing nary a nook or cranny. Often flock in great feeding swarms during the evenings. Several species may feed together.

Mating & Egg Laying: The males spend considerable time defending about 20 yards of shoreline territory. Every so often a male will drop down into the grasses and rise triumph-antly, clasping a female. Mating takes place quickly and not far from water. The female perches on an emergent plant, dipping her abdomen below the surface to insert her eggs, one at a time, into the plant's stem.

Green-striped Darner *Aeshna verticalis* (male)

MAY	JUNE	JULY	AUG	SEPT	OCT	NOV

Spring-fed waters from small lakes to slow streams. Usually associated with sedges.

Nature Notes:

The Green-striped Darner has the reputation of repeatedly hovering over the same area.

Description: Adults average 3 inches long.

Adults: The front thoracic side stripe is all green and widely notched (greater than 90 degrees ↑) with a broad rearward extension off of the top. The rear thoracic stripe is blue-green above, fading into green below in the male and all green in the female. Abdominal spots are blue in the male; female abdominal spots are mostly green, but the side spots are sometimes blue to blue-green. Female abdominal appendages are long. Claspers are of the paddle type.

Similar Species: The less-common Green-striped Darner looks maddeningly like a green-form Canada. There is no real easy way around this one, especially with the females. The front thoracic side stripe in the Green-striped is at an angle greater than 90 degrees. How much greater? Just greater. The rearward extension of the front stripe on the Green-striped is narrower than the Canada and sometimes the front stripe has a small notch in the rear margin.

If you have one in the hand you may be able to feel the Canada male's patch of tiny tooth-like bumps along the top end of the claspers (sometimes visible with a magnifier in horizontal profile). The Green-striped does not have these bumps. Abdominal appendages of the female Green-striped are longer.
Good luck!

Hunting Technique: Like the Canada Darner, they will fly almost constantly, grabbing and eating insects while in flight, often actively feeding until nightfall. They work stream edges and lakeshores systematically, missing nary a nook or a cranny.

Mating & Egg Laying: The males spend considerable time defending a territory along the water's edge. Mating takes place relatively quickly and not far from the water. The female perches on the stem of an emergent plant, dipping her abdomen below the surface to insert her eggs, one at a time, into the plant stem.

Lake Darner *Aeshna eremita* (male)

MAY	JUNE	JULY	AUG	SEPT	OCT	NOV

Bogs and lakes with marshy borders, slow streams. Less dependent on marshy waters than other blue darners.

Nature Notes:

On cool, damp, blustery September days, when nothing else seems to muster the energy to fly, the Lake Darner may still be seen going about its business.

Lake Darners normally perch vertically on tree trunks but occasionally alight on the ground.

Description: Adults average 3.1 inches long.

Adults: The front thoracic side stripe has a deep notch out of the front side (less than 90 degrees ↑). Rear thoracic side stripe has a broad but shallow notch in the front margin. Male stripes are usually green below and blue above but sometimes all blue. Female has yellow-green thoracic side stripes and abdominal top spots with blue abdominal side spots. Note the heavy black crossline on the middle of the face ↑ and the facial T-spot ↑ that has a robust upright and a top cross-piece that reaches down onto the face. Male claspers are of the paddle type and are thickened towards the end.

Similar Species: The Lake Darner is larger than the Canada, which has no black crossline on the face. Notch on Canada's front thoracic stripe is at a 90 degree angle and the Lake's is less than 90 degrees. The rear stripe of the Canada is un-notched. The less common Green-striped Darner differs in basically the same ways.

At over three inches long, the robust Lake Darner is our largest *Aeshna* species. Its range extends far to the North, reaching central Alaska, Nunavut, the Yukon and Northwest Territories.

Flight Characteristics: Look for the male's arched abdomen in flight.

Hunting Technique: Most active during the heat of the day, but it not unusual to see a few flying at dusk, joining with other blue darner species in feeding swarms.

Mating & Egg Laying: Egg laying is done in the usual blue darner way, by perching on emergent plants and inserting eggs into slits cut into submerged stems.

Larvae: Most Lake Darner nymphs reach maximum development in the summer before they emerge. During winter they enter a period of inactivity, or diapause.

Note the facial stripe and the T-spot that reaches down onto the face.

Black-tipped Darner   *Aeshna tuberculifera* (male)

MAY	JUNE	JULY	AUG	SEPT	OCT	NOV

Boggy ponds and lakes, slow vegetated streams. Prefers acidic water.

Nature Notes:

Female Black-tipped Darners may lay their eggs in plants stems high above the water's surface, sometimes as high as three feet above the waterline in cattail stems.

Description: Adults average 3 inches long.

Adults: Both thoracic side stripes are straight, of medium width and range from pale blue to light green to turquoise. Abdominal markings are blue. No black crossline on face (or a very light line) but upright portion of facial T-spot widens at base. Claspers are the paddle type ↑. In both sexes the abdomen is noticeably constricted at segment 3. Male abdominal segment 10 is black ↑. Rare yellow-form female has yellow abdominal markings.

Similar Species: Other blue-colored darners with straight thoracic side stripes have wedge-

Black-tipped Darners are named for their abdomen's entirely black segment 10. Also check out the long paddle-type claspers and obvious constriction at abdominal segment 3.

type claspers, strong black facial crossline, markings on abdominal segment 10 and thoracic side stripes that widen at the top.

Hunting Technique: The Black-tipped may be found among the darner masses in evening feeding swarms.

Mating & Egg Laying: Like the Lance-tipped Darner, the female Black-tipped has a very large ovipositor, which she uses to insert her eggs into pierced plant stems. Unlike most other blue darner species, though, these two species lay their eggs in plants stems above the water's surface. She may also lay her eggs in the mud of late summer's drying ponds. Blue form Black-tipped females have been observed displaying male behavior such as flying patrols along shorelines when they are not ready to mate. This mimicry helps them avoid unwanted male attention.

East-West Populations

There are two separate populations of the Black-tipped Darner in North America.

One population is centered around Vancouver Island on the West Coast and the other midway up the Eastern Seaboard reaching into eastern Canada and west to Minnesota.

Individuals from the two populations are indistinguishable from one another.

Shadow Darner *Aeshna umbrosa* (male)

| MAY | JUNE | JULY | AUG | SEPT | OCT | NOV |

Shaded, forested habitats. Slow streams, beaver ponds, forest bogs and ditches, preferably with rotting wood present.

Nature Notes:

There is a western sub-species of the Shadow Darner known by its scientific name, *Aeshna umbrosa occidentalis* whereas the eastern form is known as *Aeshna umbrosa umbrosa*. The western form has a more robust, and decidedly blue, mosaic pattern on the abdomen.

Description: Adults average 2.9 inches long.

Adults: Both thoracic side stripes are straight, narrow and light yellow ↑ at the bottom and blue to blue-green at the top. The top of the first stripe has a rearward extension and the bottom may widen slightly ↑. No face crossline. Abdominal markings are tiny and segment 3 is noticeably constricted. Male abdominal segment 10 is usually unmarked. Claspers are the wedge type ↑ and have a distinctive downward-pointing spur. Female abdominal appendages are narrow and rounded at the tips but commonly break off. There are green-form and blue-form females.

Most darners can be identified by carefully studying their unique thoracic stripes. Take detailed notes!

Similar Species: The Lance-tipped Darner male also has a distinctive spur on the claspers, but its abdomen is robustly patterned with larger blue spots and prefers full sunlight. The Sedge Darner has wider thoracic stripes, a heavy black crossline on the face and more patterning on the abdomen.

Hunting Technique: As its name implies, Shadow Darners hunt along shaded streams, pond edges, woodland openings and along roads until evening. They generally avoid full sunlight until late in the season when it becomes too cold for evening flight. Often found in evening feeding swarms with other darners.

Mating & Egg Laying: Males only patrol a discrete and limited section of their territory. The male clasps the female in flight, then lands. While in a horizontal position, the female deposits her eggs into the wet, rotting wood of a floating log or a partially submerged stump.

Life Cycle: In the northern portions of its range, it takes an extra year for the larvae to mature, leading to earlier emergence for those individuals the following year.

Lance-tipped **Darner** *Aeshna constricta* (male)

MAY	JUNE	JULY	AUG	SEPT	OCT	NOV

Streams, ponds, small lakes and bog pools with associated marshes and emergent vegetation.

Nature Notes:

The Lance-tipped likes to perch on grasses about a foot or so off of the ground. It is less likely to perch on tree trunks.

Description: Adults average 2.8 inches long.

Adults: The front thoracic side stripe is slightly constricted in the middle ↑. Both the front and rear stripes are wider at the top. No black crossline on the pale green face. The abdomen has a brown base, which is mostly covered with larger pale-blue spots. Female's abdomen is constricted more at segment 3 than most other blue darners. Female abdominal segment 9 is longer than segment 8 due to very long ovipositor. Male claspers are of the wedge type ↑ and have a distinctive down-pointing spur. Female abdominal appendages are lance shaped. Blue, green and yellow-form females are possible.

Lance-tipped Darners perch vertically on twigs, less often on tree trunks.

Similar Species: The closely related Shadow Darner has straight front thoracic stripes, very small abdominal top spots, smaller spurs on male claspers and narrower non-pointed female appendages. The Shadow prefers the shade; the Lance-tipped enjoys bright sunlight.

The Black-tipped male has paddle-type claspers with no spur, and no blue spots on abdominal segment 10. The female Black-tipped's thoracic side stripes are not widened at the tops, her abdominal segment 9 is not longer than segment 8, and she is almost never yellow or green.

Hunting Technique: Although it prefers sunlight, the Lance-tipped will fly until dusk, often hunting in swarms with other darners.

Mating & Egg Laying: The male gracelessly attacks the female, clasping her behind the head. They fly off in an erratic pattern, settling in low vegetation. After fertilization, the female places her eggs, one at a time, in slits she has made in the stems of tall aquatic plants such as cattail (*Typha* species) or Sweet Flag (*Acorus calamus*). Eggs may be laid as high as three feet above the water.

Lance-tipped females may be marked with green, blue or yellow. Wings of yellow females are often tinted orangish brown.

Mottled Darner *Aeshna clepsydra* (male)

MAY	JUNE	JULY	AUG	SEPT	OCT	NOV

Marsh or bog-bordered small lakes and bays of larger lakes, especially in conjunction with clear water and water-lilies.

Nature Notes:

The specific epithet, *clepsydra*, is from the Greek, *klepsydra*, which means "water clock;" this refers to the hour-glass shape of the constricted abdomen.

Description: Adults average 2.7 inches long.

Adults: As its name indicates, the thoracic side stripes are not really stripes at all but a jumble of blue, yellow and green markings ↑. The face has a brownish crossline and a heavy black facial T-spot. Male's claspers are of the paddle type ↑. Legs brown.

Similar Species: No other darner shows a colorfully mottled thorax.

Hunting Technique: Males patrol shorelines during midday, flying slowly and low to the water. May gather with other darners in evening feeding swarms along streams and in woodland openings.

Sedge Darner *Aeshna juncea* (male)

MAY	JUNE	JULY	AUG	SEPT	OCT	NOV

Bogs, ponds and marshes with sedges. Also ditches, sheltered shallow bays, rocky pools and slow streams.

Description: Adults average 2.7 inches long.

Adults: Pale blue thoracic side stripes are broad and straight ↑, the front stripe tapering only slightly at the top. The yellow face has a black crossline and a dark T-spot ↑. Male claspers are of the paddle type. Females also occur in green and yellow forms.

Similar Species: The Subarctic Darner has more-slender and curved thoracic side stripes. The Shadow Darner also has straight thoracic side stripes, but the male claspers are of the wedge type and it has no facial crossline.

Mating & Egg Laying: Female perches on a shoreline plant, dipping her abdomen in the water to insert one egg at a time into matted roots, pond-bottom muck or wet moss.

Nature Notes:

The Sedge Darner was first scientifically described in 1758 by Linnaeus in his *Systema Naturae*, which set down the foundation for our Latin-based naming system. It was listed as *Libellula juncea,* as all known dragonflies at the time were given the genus name *Libellula*.

The Sedge Darner is a northern species that just dips into the U.S.

It may take as long as four years for the larvae to mature and emerge as a dragonfly.

Variable Darner *Aeshna interrupta* (pair-male above)

MAY	JUNE	JULY	AUG	SEPT	OCT	NOV

Bog-edged waters, slow streams. Usually acidic waters.

Description: Adults average 2.9 inches long.

Nature Notes:

Variable Darners fly low to the ground with a buoyant, graceful flight.

Adults: Both thoracic side stripes are reduced and very narrow ↑. The "variable" in Variable Darner refers to the shape of the thoracic stripes, which can be a single slender Q-tip shape or a pair of streaks ↑. The stripes are usually yellow below and blue above. Abdominal spots are blue. Face has heavy black crossline and a heavy black T-spot. Claspers are of the paddle type. Female abdominal appendages are very long. Blue-form female has all blue markings and is considered rare. Green-form female has yellow thoracic stripes and green abdominal spots. Yellow-form females have all yellow markings and darker wings.

Variable Darners certainly are variable. Shown here is the whole gamut of thoracic side stripes. "Striped form" (top) shows two narrow, but complete, stripes.

In the "interrupted form" the two stripes are pinched in half with a narrow gap.

"Spotted form" has the two stripes divided into four spots.

Similar Species: There are a few western species of *Aeshna* that are very similar to the Variable Darner, but within our range it is not easily confused.

Hunting Technique: Hunts in evening feeding swarms until long after dark.

Mating & Egg Laying: Females support themselves on twigs or logs at water's edge while depositing eggs onto vertical stems of submerged plants or into the root masses of grasses.

Darners make stunning photo subjects. Patience and perseverance will pay off.

Subarctic Darner *Aeshna subarctica* (male)

MAY	JUNE	JULY	AUG	SEPT	OCT	NOV

Muskeg ponds, bogs and northern swamps.

Nature Notes:

The Subarctic Darner is a species of the Far North and is considered to be rare throughout most of its range. It's a real treat to see one.

Unlike many of the blue darner species, it does not darken if its body is cooled.

Description: Adults average 2.8 inches long.

Adults: Thoracic side stripes are uniquely bent forward at the tops ↑ and are yellow below and blue above in males and some females. Obvious black line across the yellow face ↑. T-spot is heavy and widens at its base. Male claspers are of the paddle type. Wings are clear in the blue form and may be tinted ("tea-stained") in the green and yellow form females.

Similar Species: The Sedge Darner has straight, broad thoracic side stripes. The Shadow Darner male's claspers are of the wedge type and it has no black crossline on the face.

There are very few records of Subarctic Darner in the North Woods. Its main range extends from Canada to northern and central Europe and across Siberia to Japan. It is a true circumpolar species.

Mating & Egg Laying: The female perches on an emergent plant, dipping her abdomen below the surface to insert her eggs, one at a time, into the submerged stem.

Life Cycle: Eggs mature and hatch while inside the plant stems.

Zigzag Darner *Aeshna sitchensis* (male)

MAY	JUNE	JULY	AUG	SEPT	OCT	NOV

Muskeg pools and cold sphagnum bog ponds.

Nature Notes:

The Zigzag Darner is a boreal species. It ranges across much of Canada; the southern end of its range is our North Woods.

Usually perches on the ground (as in photos above). Most blue darner species prefer to perch vertically on vegetation.

Unlike others in the genus, Zigzag Darners and Subarctic Darners are not known to feed in swarms at dusk.

Description: Adults average 2.4 inches long.

Adults: Very narrow thoracic stripes ↑ are pale blue or white; the front stripe is zigzag-shaped. The pale yellow face has a black line and a heavy T-spot with a crescent-shaped base. Abdomen has a brown base that is mostly covered with large pale blue spots. Blue-form female is blue-gray in color and green-form female is yellowish-green. Male claspers are of the paddle type.

Similar Species: The closely related Azure Darner of the far North has thicker zigzag thoracic stripes, larger abdominal spots and is smaller.

Mating & Egg Laying: Zigzag females lay eggs while perched on moss or other water-logged plants; she plunges her abdomen into the vegetation, depositing each egg.

Zigzag Darners are one of the few darners that actually prefers to perch on the ground instead of on a vertical surface.

Common Green Darner   *Anax junius* (male)

APR | MAY | JUNE | JULY | AUG | SEPT | OCT

Still waters: marshes, slow streams and permanent or temporary ponds with emergent vegetation and preferably fishless.

Nature Notes:

It has been recently postulated that, here in the North, we may have both a resident, non-migratory population and a migratory population of Green Darners. Residents overwinter here as larvae and emerge in the spring while migrating Green Darners head south in late summer. It is the offspring of these migrants that return to the North Woods in spring.

It appears as though the bulk of the fall Green Darner migration coincides with the main push of the American *(continued on next page.)*

Description: Adults average 3 inches long.

Adults: Males have an unmarked, green thorax ↑ and a bright blue abdomen. Females also have a green thorax, but her abdomen matures to a light gray. A distinctive "bull's-eye" pattern ↑ is on top of the face.

Juveniles: Both sexes also have a green thorax, but the abdomen ranges in color from dull violet to brownish-red.

Similar Species: The Eastern Pondhawk, a skimmer, is a more southerly species that may be found in the southern portion of our range. Developing juvenile male pondhawks temporarily display a green thorax and blue abdomen, but the Eastern Pondhawk is much smaller than the Green Darner and lacks the bull's-eye pattern on the face.

Flight Period: Though you may encounter Green Darners anytime in spring, summer or fall, two separate flight periods are normal. Common Green Darners are the first to be seen flying in the spring and are common until nearly midsummer; the second flight starts around early August and continues into October.

Mating & Egg Laying: Eggs are usually laid while the pair is still in tandem. The male holds the female behind the neck with his claspers while the couple lands upon emergent vegetation. The female pierces the plant below the waterline with her sharp ovipositor and inserts eggs

This recently emerged Common Green Darner shows a brick red abdomen. Females and juveniles are similarly colored.

into the stem. The female is particularly at risk of being eaten by fish during egg laying.

A competing male may try to ram another male while he is flying in tandem with a female. The aggressor's purpose is to free the female so he can mate with her.

Life Cycle: In the fall, northern juveniles migrate south en masse. Thousands of individuals flock together during the journey. They are mature by the time they reach the southern states; it is there that they lay eggs, and the offspring emerge and fly north some three months later. Among these juveniles are the first dragonflies that we will see come spring in the North Woods. They may start laying eggs even before any other species starts to emerge. Those eggs become the juveniles that leave us the same fall and fly south to continue the cycle.

(Nature Notes continued.) Kestrel migration down the North Shore of Lake Superior in Minnesota. Frank Nicoletti, the head raptor counter at Duluth's Hawk Ridge, has put forth the theory that, as kestrels are well known predators of large insects, the small falcons are using the masses of Green Darners as a fuel source during their long journey south.

Common Nighthawks also make massive fall migrations down the North Shore. But even though Green Darners feed within the same swarms of insects, I have yet to see a Nighthawk chase a Green Darner. In fact, it appears as though they feed at different altitudes.

Ocellated Darner *Boyeria grafiana* (male)

MAY	JUNE	JULY	AUG	SEPT	OCT	NOV

Lakes with rocky shorelines and clear rocky streams. Prefer waters with bowling-ball-size stones.

Nature Notes:

The Ocellated Darner will spend much of the day either hiding in dark woods or slowly patrolling rocky lakeshores and defending its territory.

They become most active during twilight.

Description: Adults average 2.6 inches long.

Adults: Both males and females have two oblong yellow thoracic spots ↑, a gray-brown body and triangular, yellow abdominal top spots. Wings have a touch of brown at their bases; wingtips are tinted brown. Eyes are green but turn partly blue in mature females. Female abdominal appendages are only as long as segment 10.

Juveniles: Young have brown eyes.

Similar Species: Fawn Darner's thoracic spots are smaller and more round than oblong.

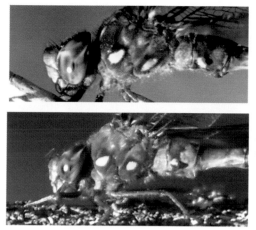

Ocellated Darner's thoracic spots are more oval to oblong.

Fawn Darner's thoracic spots are nearly round.

Flight Characteristics: Their flight, like that of the Fawn Darner is bouyant and bouncy.

Hunting Technique: Seen slowly patrolling rocky lakeshores.

Mating & Egg Laying: Egg laying and most mating behavior occurs under the cover of darkness.

Fawn Darner *Boyeria vinosa* (male)

MAY	JUNE	JULY	AUG	SEPT	OCT	NOV

Ranges along very small streams to larger rivers, usually shaded. Occasionally found along lakes with bare shorelines

Nature Notes:

Fawn Darners are very inquisitive and will inspect every little detail of their environment, even the dragonfly enthusiast.

Fawn Darners are sometimes seen flying with Ocellated Darners.

Description: Adults average 2.6 inches long.

Adults: Both male and female have two small, yellow thoracic spots ↑, a brownish body and muted or absent abdominal spots ↑. Female abdominal appendages are longer than abdominal segment 10.

Juveniles: Young Fawn Darners have olive-brown eyes.

Similar Species: Ocellated Darners have larger more oval thoracic spots and the female's abdominal appendages are shorter.

Flight Characteristics: Their flight, like that of the Ocellated Darner, is bouyant and bouncy, more reminiscent of a damselfly than a dragonfly.

Fawn Darners become most active just before dusk. Though not adverse to flying during the day, they seem to prefer evening hunts.

Hunting Technique: The Fawn Darner will spend much of the day either hiding in dark, shaded places or slowly patrolling streams and rivulets. They become most active at dusk.

Mating & Egg Laying: Egg laying and most mating behaviors occur under the protective darkness of night.

Larvae: Usually found under bark, leaves and wood in streams and rivers.

Cyrano Darner   *Nasiaeschna pentacantha* (male)

MAY	JUNE	JULY	AUG	SEPT	OCT	NOV

Sheltered bays, slow woodland streams and ponds. Prefers bottoms made up of sticks, twigs and rotting leaf debris.

Nature Notes:

Aptly named for the nasally-endowed fictional character, Cyrano de Bergerac. (How about "*Shnozz-iaeschna*" instead of *Nasiaeschna*?)

Much of the North Woods is at or above the northernmost range of the Cyrano, but look for it in our southern regions.

Unlike many other darners, they do not swarm.

Males patrol very regular territories along woodland edges and over ponds and streams.

Description: Adults average 2.7 inches long.

Adults: Blue-green face with prominent frons or "nose" ↑, bright blue eyes and jagged thoracic side stripes of green. Male has thick, tapering abdomen; the female's is thick and untapering. Abdominal markings of bold green patterns. Short abdominal appendages in both sexes.

Similar Species: The female green-form Springtime Darner has a noticeable constriction at segment 3 of her abdomen.

Flight Characteristics: Male's patrolling flight is slow and deliberate, with wings held in an unusually high position.

Mating & Egg Laying: Females lay eggs in rotting wood in the shade.

Harlequin Darner *Gomphaeschna furcillata* (male)

MAY	JUNE	JULY	AUG	SEPT	OCT	NOV

Sphagnum bog ponds surrounded by woods. Also alder swamps.

Description: Adults average 2.2 inches long.

Adults: Our smallest darner ↑. Thorax is greenish brown with several cream-colored side stripes. Abdomen is black with green spots on segments 2 to 9. Green eyes ↑. Male's lower abdominal appendages (the epiproct) are deeply forked. Female has white side spots and orangish top spots, forewings with an orange smudge near the tip and very short abdominal appendages. Wings of both sexes sparsely veined.

Similar Species: None are this small.

Hunting Technique: Feed along wooded openings. Males sometimes congregate with other males in feeding swarms.

Mating & Egg Laying: Females lay eggs in rotting wood near mats of sphagnum moss.

Nature Notes:

Males patrol small territories over the sphagnum moss beds where "their" females lay eggs. Territorial males often face down intruding males while hovering.

Swamp Darner *Epiaeschna heros* (male)

| MAY | JUNE | JULY | AUG | SEPT | OCT | NOV |

Shaded woodland streams, pools and swamps.

Nature Notes:

The large Swamp Darner is found in the southern regions of the North Woods.

Occasionally migrates in massive swarms.

This is the only species in genus *Epiaeschna*.

Description: Adults average 3.4 inches long.

Adults: Huge and brown with green thoracic stripes and green abdominal rings ↑. The female has leaf-shaped abdominal appendages (cerci). Wings may be tinted ("tea-stained"). Their head is very broad. Eyes are bright blue.

Similar Species: No other darner is brown with green abdomen rings.

Hunting Technique: They often feed away from water, sometimes gathering to feed on swarms of flying-ants. The Swamp Darner will enter buildings when hunting.

Mating & Egg Laying: Males are not territorial. Females insert eggs into muddy banks, rotten wood or plant stems. Eggs are also laid in dry pond bottoms.

Springtime Darner *Basiaeschna janata* (male)

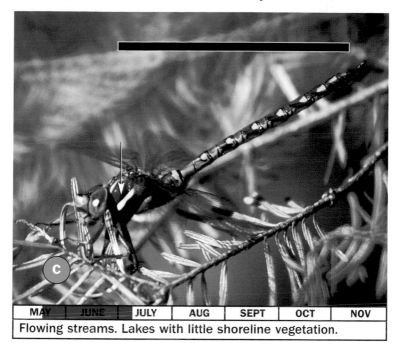

MAY	JUNE	JULY	AUG	SEPT	OCT	NOV

Flowing streams. Lakes with little shoreline vegetation.

Description: Adults average 2.4 inches long.

Adults: Two pale yellow side stripes on brown thorax ↑, blue eyes and a small dark brown spot at the base of each wing. Male abdominal spots are blue; female spots are either blue or green. Female abdominal appendages are as long as segments 9 plus 10.

Similar Species: Most darners emerge later in the summer than the Springtime Darner.

Flight Characteristics: Males patrol an irregular beat, following the shoreline. Along streams, they may bounce from bank to bank.

Hunting Technique: They will hunt in the shade and into the darkness of evening.

Mating & Egg Laying: Female lays eggs in submerged aquatic plants by puncturing the stem with her ovipositor in a zig-zag pattern —much like a sewing machine—leaving a double row of eggs behind.

Nature Notes:

Our earliest darner to emerge in the spring; it is often on the wing by mid May.

Clubtails
Family Gomphidae

The clubtails are our only family of dragonflies with eyes that do not meet at the top of the head. (The Petaltail family (Petaluridae) also has separated eyes, but they are not found in the North Woods.) In this regard, their heads look very much like a damselfly's. Most clubtails are yellow and black, medium in size and have some degree of swelling, or club, at the end of the abdomen. The wings are without dark patches and the forewing and hindwing triangles are similar in size.

Shortly after the male clasps the female for mating they perch several minutes to complete copulation, then separate. The females lack an ovipositor or have a very reduced one. Eggs are usually laid in moving water without the male guarding nearby. Larval clubtails, in general, demand water with a high oxygen content, which restricts most species to clean, faster-flowing rivers and streams.

The clubtails are primarily ground perchers. They hunt from this position, flying short sorties after prey then coming again to perch.

There are 28 species of clubtails in the North Woods, 98 species in North America and an estimated 1,000 species worldwide.

The Snaketails — Genus *Ophiogomphus*

The snaketails are named for their linear abdominal markings (*ophis* means "serpent"). The thorax is usually bright green. They are sturdy, plucky dragonflies of medium size with short legs. Author and odonatist Sid Dunkle aptly refers to the snaketails as the "trout" of the dragonfly world; they are beautiful creatures with a reliance on pristine waters. The nymphs burrow in sand but are vulnerable to being buried in silt from erosion or washed away during spring snowmelt.

Cruising snaketails virtually disappear as they fly about a foot over glistening riffles, their wings reflecting the glimmering sunlight just like the water. Females lay eggs in these rapids by coyly dipping the tips of their abdomens in the rushing water.

In just the last few years there have been two very exciting discoveries within the genus *Ophiogomphus*; odonatists have found two new species in Wisconsin (Sand Snaketail and Wisconsin Snaketail) and are searching for them in similar habitats in Minnesota. Are there more undescribed species out there? Get out and start looking!

Dragonhunters (Genus *Hagenius*)
58 Dragonhunter

Common Clubtails (Genus *Gomphus*)

Subgenus *Gomphus*
60 Green-faced Clubtail
61 Mustached Clubtail

Subgenus *Phanogomphus*
62 Dusky Clubtail
64 Ashy Clubtail
65 Lancet Clubtail
66 Rapids Clubtail
68 Pronghorn Clubtail

Subgenus *Gomphurus*
69 Cobra Clubtail
70 Skillet Clubtail
72 Midland Clubtail
73 Splendid Clubtail

Hanging Clubtails (Genus *Stylurus*)
74 Arrow Clubtail
75 Elusive Clubtail
76 Riverine Clubtail
77 Zebra Clubtail

Spinylegs (Genus *Dromogomphus*)
78 Black-shouldered Spinyleg

Pond Clubtails (Genus *Arigomphus*)
80 Horned Clubtail
81 Lilypad Clubtail

Least Clubtails (Genus *Stylogomphus*)
82 Least Clubtail

Sanddragons (Genus *Progomphus*)
83 Common Sanddragon

Snaketails (Genus *Ophiogomphus*)
84 Boreal Snaketail
86 Extra-striped Snaketail
87 Pygmy Snaketail
88 Riffle Snaketail
89 Rusty Snaketail
90 Wisconsin Snaketail
91 Sand Snaketail

Dragonhunter *Hagenius brevistylus* (male)

MAY	JUNE	JULY	AUG	SEPT	OCT	NOV

Moderate- to swift-flowing forest rivers and streams.

Nature Notes:

In the entire world there is only one member of the genus *Hagenius*...the legendary Dragonhunter!

The Dragonhunter seems immune to the effects of certain wasp stings and the toxins that build up in the Monarch butterflies that they eat.

Description: Adults average 3.3 inches long.

Adults: Huge dragonfly with powerful legs and a large thorax ↑. Black and yellow markings. Two large, yellow thoracic stripes. Green eyes, black-striped yellow face and a small head. Occiput black. Legs entirely black and very long with short, heavy spines ↑ on the tibiae (long, lower-leg sections) that assist in taking large prey. Wing triangles are elongated and angular on the outer side. Abdominal segments 9 and 10 are completely black on top; the rest show some yellow. Wings are coarse to the touch and slightly tinted.

Similar Species: There is no other black-and-yellow dragonfly as large as the Dragonhunter.

Flight Characteristics: Flies with abdomen curled under. Silhouette looks like sideways "J."

Hunting Technique: Like its name implies, the Dragonhunter is a fierce predator and has

The Dragonhunter is a legendary insect. It is on the "most wanted" list of many dragonfly enthusiasts. I have witnessed its power through a seasoned German odonatist, his hands trembling as he held his first Dragonhunter.

been known to eat large butterflies (like swallowtails) and even other dragonflies—including fellow Dragonhunters! They usually attack from above and will sometimes knock prey into the water before coming in for the kill.

Mating & Egg Laying: Dragonhunters rarely fly in tandem when mating. (The male's claspers sometimes, inexplicably, puncture the female's head during mating.) She dips her abdomen into water while flying over small pools to deposit eggs.

Larvae: The aquatic nymph's abdomen is large, leaf-shaped and flattened. They hide in leaf-litter that settles in stream eddies. Mature larvae prefer sheltered shorelines with sandy bottoms. All other clubtail larvae are burrowers. The larvae of the Stream Cruiser family (Macromiidae) have similar, petal-shaped abdomens.

Riverside rocks are convenient perches from which to launch their patrolling runs.

Green-faced Clubtail   *Gomphus viridifrons* (male)

| MA... | ...LY | AUG | SEPT | OCT | NOV |

Medium streams to small rivers with rapids and riffles. Prefers clean, clear waters with a mixed substrate of gravel and silt.

Description: Adults average 1.8 inches long.

Adults: Yellow face with only light markings along the sutures. Missing the middle side stripe on the thorax that is present in many other clubtails. Male has tiny yellow top spots ↑; female top spots are small but larger than the male's. No top spots on segments 8 to10 ↑. Segment 9 is shorter than segment 8 in both sexes. Abdomen forms a noticeable club.

Similar Species: The Mustached Clubtail has darker facial outlining. The Rapids Clubtail has a middle thoracic stripe, a slight abdominal club and segment 9 is as long or is longer than segment 8.

Mating & Egg Laying: Eggs are laid in fast water. The eggs are washed into slower pools where the larvae will develop.

Nature Notes:

The Green-faced Clubtail is most active in the late afternoon and under cloud cover.

Seldom found in great numbers, it is considered rare over most of its range.

Mustached Clubtail *Gomphus adelphus* (female)

| MAY | JUNE | JULY | AUG | SEPT | OCT | NOV |

Small streams to small rivers with rapids and riffles. Usually in clean, clear waters. Also found in lakes with exposed shorelines.

Description: Adults average 1.7 inches long.

Adults: Yellow face with thick black outlining of facial sutures ↑. Occiput is yellow with black corners. They lack the middle side stripe on the thorax that is present on many other Clubtails. Male has tiny, yellow abdominal top spots; female top spots are small but are larger than the male's. No top spots on segments 8 to 10. Segment 9 is shorter than segment 8 in both sexes. Abdomen forms a noticeable club.

Similar Species: The Green-faced has much lighter facial outlining. The Rapids Clubtail has a middle thoracic stripe, only a slightly expanded abdominal club and segment 9 is as long, or longer, than segment 8.

Mating & Egg Laying: Eggs are laid in rushing water that washes them into pools below. This is where the larvae will develop.

Nature Notes:

The Mustached Clubtail is most active in the late afternoon.

Dusky Clubtail *Gomphus spicatus* (male)

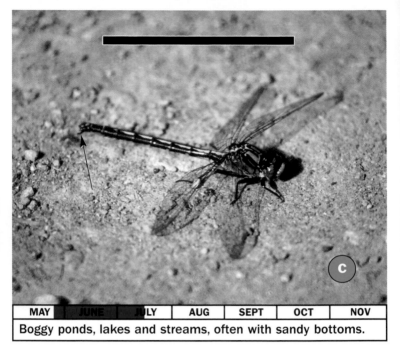

| MAY | JUNE | JULY | AUG | SEPT | OCT | NOV |

Boggy ponds, lakes and streams, often with sandy bottoms.

Nature Notes:

When not actively engaged in oviposition, Duskies are likely found far from water, perched in the sunshine on gravel roads, trails or rocks.

Dusky, Ashy and Lancet Clubtails can be observed flying in a series of incomplete loops.

Description: Adults average 2 inches long.

Adults: Coloration is dull and "dusky." The narrow abdomen shows little clubbing and yellow lance-like markings to segment 7, a small spot on 8, no marks on 9 ↑ and a dull yellow stripe down the center of 10 (especially in the female). Male's clasper has a downward-pointing "tooth" ↑. Female occiput is convex ↑ and bumpy. Female eye color is gray above and darker below.

Similar Species: The Ashy Clubtail's clasper does not have the downward-pointing tooth of the Dusky. The female Ashy can have violet-colored eyes; female Dusky never does. The Lancet Clubtail is smaller, has a definite club and usually has better defined markings near the end of the abdomen.

Hunting Technique: The Dusky will feed on damselflies when hunting near the water.

From this angle you can clearly see that abdominal segment 9 is unmarked and segment 10 has a yellow stripe.

Larvae: The aquatic nymph lives on a substrate made up of mostly detritus. When emerging, the nymph may not completely leave the water before undergoing transformation to adulthood. Therefore, after a large emergence, it is not uncommon for the exuviae to be found floating in the water instead of clinging to the shoreline.

Note the distinctive convex profile of the female's occiput. The closely related Ashy female has a concave occiput.

Ashy Clubtail *Gomphus lividus* (male)

| MAY | JUNE | JULY | AUG | SEPT | OCT | NOV |

Small to large streams with gentle current. Sheltered shore-lines of large lakes (with scant vegetation and shallow water).

Nature Notes:

Ashy, Lancet and Dusky Clubtails can be observed flying in a series of partial loops.

Description: Adults average 2 inches long.

Adults: Coloration is dull and "ashy." Narrow abdomen with little clubbing. Abdominal segment 8 has a yellow triangular spot on top ↑; segments 9 and 10 are brown above. May show a black facial crossline. Male's claspers lack a down-pointing "tooth." Female eye color ranges from gray-brown to violet, and her occiput is concave with no bumps.

Similar Species: The Dusky Clubtail is very similar, but his clasper has a down-pointing tooth. The female Dusky does not normally have violet-colored eyes. The Lancet Clubtail is smaller, has a pronounced club and yellow markings on abdomen segments 9 and 10.

Larvae: The nymph lives on the muddy or sandy bottoms of slow-flowing streams and large lakes.

Lancet Clubtail *Gomphus exilis* (male)

MAY	JUNE	JULY	AUG	SEPT	OCT	NOV

Marshy ponds, sand-bottomed lakes and slow streams, usually with floating and non-emergent vegetation.

Description: Adults average 1.7 inches long.

Adults: Abdomen moderately clubbed with yellow lance-shaped spots to segment 8 and broad yellow markings on top of segments 9 and 10. Outer edges of segments 8 and 9 have bright yellow patches ↑ that are visible in flight. Thorax is greenish-yellow with dark, mid-dorsal stripes that widen at the bottom into a broad triangle. Female occiput is slightly notched at its center. Male claspers lancet-shaped.

Similar Species: The Ashy and Dusky Clubtails have smaller clubs and larger bodies. The Pronghorn Clubtail has a larger club.

Mating & Egg Laying: Female lays eggs in open water, touching the tip of her abdomen to the surface every few feet.

Larvae: The aquatic nymph prefers marshy edges where there is a current or waves.

Nature Notes:

Disturbed Lancets will dart away in an undulating flight and land ten or so feet up in a tree.

The Lancet Clubtail is a bold little species. While swimming with my family north of Duluth, we found ourselves the preferred perch for dozens of Lancets. There were several at a time on each of us!

Rapids Clubtail *Gomphus quadricolor* (female)

| MAY | JUNE | JULY | AUG | SEPT | OCT | NOV |

Large, rocky streams and rivers. Pools below gravelly, rock-studded riffles. Occasionally around slower, weedy, streams.

Nature Notes:

The aquatic nymphs crawl out of the water into dense stands of semi-aquatic plants to emerge. The exuviae can be very difficult to find, as emergence takes place in thick shoreline vegetation.

Description: Adults average 1.7 inches long.

Adults: Abdomen blackish with linear, yellow top spots; segments 8 to 10 unmarked above ↑. Side spots of segments 8 to 10 are brighter yellow. Segments 8 and 9 are of equal length. Thorax is black with several yellow stripes. Claspers and legs are all black.

Similar Species: The larger Dusky Clubtail is duller, has light-colored stripes on the legs and has yellow top spots on segments 8 and 10.

Mating & Egg Laying: Females lay their eggs in swift moving waters so their eggs are washed down to quiet pools where the nymphs will develop.

Rapids Clubtails perch on the ground or low vegetation when away from water. Along the fast flowing streams they prefer, they perch on shoreline rocks or even boulders in the middle of the rapids.

Pronghorn Clubtail *Gomphus graslinellus* (male)

MAY	JUNE	JULY	AUG	SEPT	OCT	NOV

Lakes, ponds and sluggish streams.

Nature Notes:

Unlike similar species, the Pronghorn Clubtail does not hover over fast water and riffles. It prefers to perch on rocky shorelines near the largest pools, waiting to spot potential prey.

Description: Adults average 2 inches long.

Adults: Abdomen is black with bright yellow markings. The sides of segments 8 and 9 are heavily marked with yellow; segment 8 has a smaller top spot and segment 9 is all yellow on top (except for the female's top spot which is narrower). Segment 10 has a narrow stripe. Upper male abdominal appendages (cerci) each have a tooth extending outwards ↑, reminiscent of the horns on a Pronghorn Antelope.

Similar Species: The larger Plains Clubtail spends its time patrolling over fast water and riffles and lacks the prominent outward tooth on the cerci.

Larvae: Aquatic nymphs crawl out of the water into dense stands of semi-aquatic plants to emerge. The exuviae is usually found muddied and lying on the ground.

Cobra Clubtail *Gomphus vastus* (male)

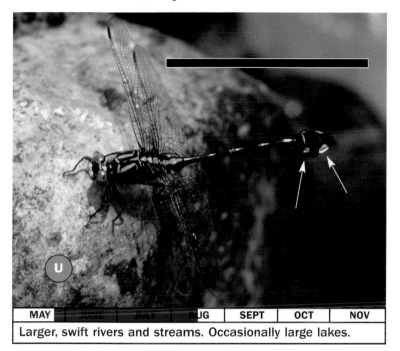

| MAY | JUNE | JULY | AUG | SEPT | OCT | NOV |

Larger, swift rivers and streams. Occasionally large lakes.

Description: Adults average 2.1 inches long.

Adults: Broad, clubbed abdomen is as wide as the thorax. Very narrow from segments 3 to 6. Yellow abdominal side spot on segment 8 is smaller than side spot on segment 9 ↑; smaller spot of segment 8 does not reach the lower edge of the club whereas the larger spot of 9 does reach the edge with no black margin ↑. No yellow top spots on segments 8 to 10. Black facial stripes. Eyes usually dark green. Inner margins of the wings may be slightly tea-stained.

Similar Species: Skillet Clubtails have an even wider club and a larger side spot on segment 8.

Mating & Egg Laying: Female flies far out into open water (river or lake) to let waves wash accumulated blobs of eggs off her abdomen.

Nature Notes:

Cobra Clubtails perch on shoreline brush, sand or rocks.

Skillet Clubtail *Gomphus ventricosus* (male)

MAY	JUNE	JULY	AUG	SEPT	OCT	NOV

Fast-flowing larger streams and rivers. Also sandy or calcium-rich clay-bottomed larger lakes with good water quality.

Nature Notes:

The strikingly beautiful Skillet Clubtail has the dual distinction of being the smallest of the Subgenus *Gomphurus* and of having the largest club of any of the Clubtails (thus the moniker—skillet).

Often hidden low in vegetation or on the ground.

Description: Adults average 1.9 inches long.

Adults: Huge skillet-sized club (segments 7 to 10) is wider than the thorax ↑. Yellow abdominal side spots on segments 8 and 9 are very close to each other ↑ (sometimes small spots on 7 and 10 as well). Side spot on segment 8 has a distinct black rim, and there is no top spot on segments 8 to 10 (or rarely a small dot on 8 or 10). Yellow top spots form a broken line that ends with a narrow triangle on segment 7. The unstriped thorax is greenish-yellow with a distinct black stripe on the shoulder. No facial crossline.

Similar Species: The larger Midland has a club narrower than its thorax, a top spot on segment 8 and the side spot on 8 reaches the edge without a black rim. All other clubtails with broad clubs have thoracic side stripes.

We could nickname this dragonfly the "flying frying pan." Enlarged abdominal segments 7 to 10 are skillet-sized and wider than its thorax.

Flight Characteristics: Bouncy flight.

Hunting Technique: Males patrol over open water in quick, bouncy little jaunts, only to return quickly to a favored perch.

Midland Clubtail *Gomphus fraternus* (male)

MAY		AUG	SEPT	OCT	NOV

Fast-flowing larger streams and the shallows of large lakes where there is plenty of wave action. Prefers clear, hard water.

Nature Notes:

Strong flight allows them to prey on other dragonflies such as the Twelve-spotted Skimmer and Eastern Pondhawk.

The aquatic nymph burrows into clay or sand bottoms, sometimes in very deep water.

Description: Adults average 2.2 inches long.

Adults: Large abdomen club is only slightly narrower than the thorax. Yellow, lancet-shaped spots to segment 7 and a small yellow triangle on segment 8 ↑; segments 9 and 10 have no topside markings. Yellow spots on the sides of segments 8 and 9 ↑. No black crossline on face.

Similar Species: The larger Splendid Clubtail has a black facial crossline and no triangle on segment 9.

Flight Characteristics: Very strong flyers.

Hunting Technique: Strong flight allows them to chase down other dragonflies including Twelve-spotted Skimmer and Eastern Pondhawk.

Mating & Egg Laying: Females lay eggs by washing them off their abdomen in splashing rapids or waves. Males undertake swift, long patrols over riffles and far out over water.

Splendid Clubtail *Gomphus lineatifrons* (male)

MAY	JUNE	JULY	AUG	SEPT	OCT	NOV

Clean, gravel-bottomed, medium to large rivers with fast flowing rocky sections.

Description: Adults average 2.6 inches long.

Adults: One of our larger Clubtails. Broad club at end of the abdomen is NOT wider than its thorax. Sides of the club are flattened and form vertical sides. Just a small splotch of yellow on the side of segment 7, but larger yellow patches on the sides of segments 8 and 9 touch the front edges of the segments. Narrow yellow top spots up to segment 7. Segment 8 usually without top spot, or with very small yellow spot. Segment 10 and legs are all black. Black crossline on yellow face ↑. Bright green eyes ↑.

Similar Species: The Midland Clubtail has a top spot on segment 8 and lacks the black facial crossline. The Skillet and the Cobra Clubtails have a side spot on segment 8 that is enclosed in black and does not reach the forward edge of the segment.

Nature Notes:

This large Clubtail is not the most graceful of the Odonata, but with its size and large, flared club it strikes an imposing figure when in flight.

Splendid Clubtails hesitate to spend much time on the wing in cooler weather, preferring the warmth of direct sunlight.

While perched on the ground, Splendids will turn around by walking instead of flying.

Arrow Clubtail *Stylurus spiniceps* (male)

MAY	JUNE	JULY	AUG	SEPT	OCT	NOV

Sandy-bottomed larger rivers. Occasionally found along smaller rivers or lakes.

Nature Notes:

The Arrow Clubtail is a strong flyer that is known to fly until dark, or later.

Members of the *Stylurus* or "hanging clubtails" often perch on the top of leaves; the leaf sagging under their weight.

Description: Adults average 2.5 inches long.

Adults: Large and long for a *Stylurus.* Overall black dragonfly with very light yellow-green markings. The thoracic side stripes are so heavy that they almost merge to one ↑. Abdominal segments 8 and 9 (sometimes only 9) have light yellow side spots. Segment 9 is noticeably longer than 8 ↑. Face and legs are black. Female has a pair of large "horns" on her occiput. Eyes green.

Similar Species: Elusive Clubtail has narrower thoracic stripes and blue eyes.

Flight Characteristics: Strong flyer.

Mating & Egg Laying: Egg laying occurs in rapids.

Elusive Clubtail *Stylurus notatus* (male)

MAY	JUNE	JULY	AUG	SEPT	OCT	NOV

Large lakes and bigger rivers with sandy bottoms.

Description: Adults average 2.4 inches long.

Adults: Two black thoracic side stripes on a yellow background. Abdominal top spots are very small on segments 4 to 6, broader in 7 and 8 and absent, or greatly reduced, in 9 and 10. Yellow side spots on segments 7 to 10; those on 8 and 9 are larger ↑. Upper part of male's face is black. Moderately clubbed tail. Blue eyes ↑.

Similar Species: This is the only species of similar description with blue eyes. The Riverine Clubtail has a thoracic "star" in front of the wings. The Arrow Clubtail's abdominal segment 9 is longer than 8.

Flight Characteristics: Flies long, swooping forays far out over open water.

Mating & Egg Laying: Females descend from their flights over open water to deposit eggs into the lake.

Nature Notes:

The Elusive Clubtail is aptly named, as it is considered nearly uncatchable by net-wielding enthusiasts. It flies long, swooping forays far out over open water, and when it does perch, it is high up in nearby trees.

Numbers locally may be great, as indicated by the presence of many exuviae, but the adults are seldom seen.

Riverine Clubtail *Stylurus amnicola* (male)

MAY	JUNE	JULY	AUG	SEPT	OCT	NOV

Swift-running medium to large rivers with sand, gravel or mud.

Nature Notes:

The Riverine Clubtail is not as wary as our other hanging clubtails.

Description: Adults average 2.1 inches long.

Adults: It is the smallest *Stylurus* species but has the biggest club. On top of the thorax is a yellow triangle in between the two yellow stripes. Rearward thoracic stripes are reduced to several interrupted black side stripes. Abdominal segments 8 and 9 have broad yellow side spots that do not reach the edge ↑. Eyes green. Legs black with yellow hind thighs.

Similar Species: Other species of *Stylurus* are larger and do not have a three-pointed star on the front of their thorax. The much larger Black-shouldered Spinyleg has a similarly patterned thorax, but it has very long legs with obvious spines.

Hunting Technique: Males patrol during the middle of the day, often over the middles of rivers. Forages from perches in the undergrowth, either in sun or shade.

Zebra Clubtail *Stylurus scudderi* (male)

| MAY | JUNE | JULY | AUG | SEPT | OCT | NOV |

Cool, fast-flowing streams and smaller rivers with sandy bottoms.

Description: Adults average 2.3 inches long.

Adults: Black with bright yellow markings. Stripes on top of thorax are skinny, yellow ovals completely surrounded by black ↑. Abdominal segments 3 to 7 are ringed in yellow ↑. Segments 7 to 9 have small triangular top spots. Male has a broad club; female has a stout, but non clubbed, abdomen.

Similar Species: The bold black-and-yellow rings makes this dragonfly unique.

Hunting Technique: From low perches, the male makes short patrolling flights over riffles.

Nature Notes:

The Zebra Clubtail is a very wary creature, especially females, which are almost never captured or observed.

Transformation to adulthood usually takes place during midday instead of in the early morning, as is common with most dragonflies.

Black-shouldered Spinyleg
Dromogomphus spinosus (female)

MAY	JUNE	JULY	AUG	SEPT	OCT	NOV

Streams, rivers and large lakes with rocky shores. Will tolerate muddy rivers but larvae will not be found in acidic waters.

Nature Notes:

Even if emergence begins in early June, bright yellow juveniles may be found as late as the end of July. By late summer, the Black-shouldered Spinyleg may be one of the few club-tails still on the wing.

Description: Adults average 2.5 inches long.

Adults: The name just about says it all; they have a wide, black shoulder-stripe ↑ on the yellow to olive thorax and numerous spines ↑ on the thigh of the long hind leg. Small head in relation to the rest of the body. Vivid green eyes. Top of the thorax (between the head and the wings) has distinctive markings consisting of two long, yellow ovals separated by a wide, pale I-shaped stripe ↑.

Juveniles: As with most clubtails, the young are more striking than the adults with their bright yellow markings.

Similar Species: None. Size, shape and colors are distinctive.

Mating & Egg Laying: Black-shouldered Spinylegs may finish copulation high up in the treetops. The female lays eggs alone as she

This photo clearly shows that the male's abdomen is distinctly clubbed; the female's abdomen barely widens at the tip.

skims above the water's surface at considerable speed. Without slowing down, she drops the tip of her abdomen to the water and deposits an egg every few feet.

Larvae: Black-shouldered Spinyleg larvae are similar in appearance to the

Long leg spines aid in capturing and holding prey.

larvae of Pronghorn Clubtails and Ashy Clubtails, suggesting that, despite a considerable difference in the way the adults look, the species may be closely related.

Mature adults are more pale than juveniles. The shiny yellow fades to a pale blue-green over time.

Horned Clubtail *Arigomphus cornutus* (female)

| MAY | JUNE | JULY | AUG | SEPT | OCT | NOV |

Slow-moving, small- to medium-size streams, often with marshy or boggy edges. Also about small, muddy ponds.

Nature Notes:

The Horned Clubtail is very wary. It seems to like to perch on lily pads, just out of net's reach.

They are agile flyers.

Description: Adults average 2.2 inches long.

Adults: The abdomen is black with long, skinny, yellowish triangular top spots (only segment 9 has no top spot). It is the only male Gomphid in its range with abdominal segment 10 wider than segment 9. A thoracic top stripe connects with the thinner shoulder stripe in both sexes. Females have a high yellow cleft occiput ↑ (see inset photo), which is unmistakable; female has two small, yellow horn-like protuberances located just behind the eyes and the occiput. Males have very distinct, widely-forked claspers that are greenish with black tips.

Similar Species: The Lilypad Clubtail is closely related, but it has no abdominal top spot on segments 8 or 9.

Lilypad Clubtail *Arigomphus furcifer* (male)

MAY	JUNE	JULY	AUG	SEPT	OCT	NOV

Marshy ponds, lakes and slow streams; usually with water-lily pads and brushy shores. Also bog ponds and lakes.

Description: Adults average 2 inches long.

Adults: Long, thin, yellowish triangular top spots on all abdomen segments except 8 and 9 ↑. Rusty borders on sides of segments 8 and 9. The male has distinctive gold claspers with inward-pointing spikes. Thorax is gray-green with thin top stripes. Legs black. Azure eyes ↑.

Similar Species: The Horned Clubtail has a wider abdomen with a top spot on segment 8. The female Horned has a very high occiput. Snaketails are brighter green. The Black-shouldered Spinyleg has awesome spines projecting from its femurs and a broader, black shoulder stripe.

Mating & Egg Laying: The female lays eggs by tapping the water with the tip of her abdomen every five seconds; she flies erratically in between egg laying bouts.

Nature Notes:

The aquatic nymph often crawls up on floating vegetation, such as water lilies, to transform into adulthood. When shoreline vegetation is chosen, it rarely crawls completely out of the water before emerging.

They perch on small trees, floating vegetation and occasionally the ground.

Least Clubtail *Stylogomphus albistylus* (male)

MAY	JUNE	JULY	AUG	SEPT	OCT	NOV

Cool, fast-flowing streams and smaller rivers, with sandy bottoms and projecting stones.

Nature Notes:

The Least Clubtail is a very wary creature.

They fly quickly just above the water, darting up into overhanging trees and shrubs to take cover.

Males perch on exposed stones.

Description: Adults average 1.5 inches long.

Adults: A tiny clubtail ↑. The thorax is dark with pale-green stripes (or pale-green with dark stripes). Pale yellow abdominal side spots on segments 4 to 7 are often connected, forming rings around the abdomen. Note the male's white claspers ↑. Vivid green eyes ↑.

Similar Species: None.

Flight Characteristics: They fly very quickly and close to the water.

Mating & Egg Laying: Egg laying takes place amongst the rapids and exposed rocks.

Common Sanddragon *Progomphus obscurus* (male)

MAY	JUNE	JULY	AUG	SEPT	OCT	NOV

Sand-bottomed streams, rivers and larger lakes.

Description: Adults average 2 inches long.

Adults: Thorax is striped with yellow and brown in about equal proportions. Wings show a small brown spot at the base and the leading vein is yellow ↑. Irregular abdominal top spots from segments 2 through 7, none on segments 8 to 10. Small yellow spot on hind legs near femur-tibia joint. Male has green-yellow eyes, and female has brown eyes. Male and female abdominal appendages are yellow ↑.

Similar Species: None.

Mating & Egg Laying: The male and female are in tandem for ten to fifteen minutes while fertilization takes place. The Common Sand-dragon is the only clubtail species in which the female is guarded during egg laying. Eggs are laid in shallows along stream pool edges.

Nature Notes:

Males are most active during midday, making forays over lakes.

Males perch in the open, on the ground or on the tips of twigs or grasses.

Boreal Snaketail *Ophiogomphus colubrinus* (male)

| MAY | JUNE | JULY | AUG | SEPT | OCT | NOV |

Clear and cold fast-flowing streams with gravelly bottoms.

Description: Adults average 1.9 inches long.

Adults: Bright green thorax with dark side stripes. Face and occiput are green ↑ with a heavy black crossline on face. The clubbed abdomen is mostly dark brown (not black) with pale yellow markings that become smaller and more T-shaped from segment 3 to 7 ↑. Segment 8's top spot is shaped like a long rectangle with a thin tail; segment 9 and 10 top spots are more oval with similar tails. Side spots on segments 7 to 9 and only a wash of yellow on the side of 10. Legs black with pale thighs. Female has a pair of small brown occipital horns.

Similar Species: The smaller Extra-striped Snaketail has an interruption of the lower, upward-arching facial crossline, black legs and an N-shaped set of side stripes on the thorax.

Nature Notes:

The Boreal Snaketail has the largest club of all of our snaketails, which really isn't all that big compared to other clubtails. It also has the northernmost range of the Clubtail family.

They prefer to perch low, often on the ground or in bushes. The juveniles, when away from water, will perch on twigs in the canopy.

Teneral (newly emerged) Boreal Snaketail preparing for its first flight. Note the empty larval case (exuviae) below the dragonfly.

Flight Characteristics: Undulating flight interrupted by hovering.

Hunting Technique: Males patrol broad areas of moving water.

Larvae: The aquatic nymphs burrow shallowly in sandy stream bottoms.

Young Boreal Snaketails are very pale. The colors will deepen with age.

Extra-striped Snaketail *Ophiogomphus anomalus* (male)

MAY	JUNE	JULY	AUG	SEPT	OCT	NOV

Clear, cold, medium-size rivers.

Nature Notes:

The Extra-striped Snaketail is fairly uncommon and local.

The Extra-striped Snaketail spends much of its time aloft and rarely perches low or on rocks.

Aquatic nymphs burrow shallowly in sandy river bottoms.

Description: Adults average 1.7 inches long.

Adults: Bright green thorax with side stripes, which form a conspicuous N-shape ↑ just above the leg bases. Face and occiput are green. Heavy black crosslines on face with the upward-arching lower line interrupted. Female has a pair of small, upright, black "horns" in the center of the occiput. Abdomen is mostly black with long, yellow top spots; spots on 7 and 8 are shorter. Segments 9 and 10 each show a round spot. Sides of segments 7 to 10 with variously shaped yellow spots. Legs black.

Similar Species: The Boreal Snaketail has pale thighs, not black. Other snaketail species have the upper portion of the front thoracic stripe missing. The Rapids Clubtail has no markings on abdominal segments 8 or 9.

Pygmy Snaketail *Ophiogomphus howei* (male)

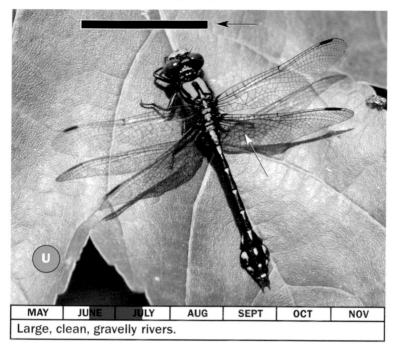

MAY	JUNE	JULY	AUG	SEPT	OCT	NOV

Large, clean, gravelly rivers.

Description: Adults average 1.3 inches long.

Adults: Very small for a snaketail ↑. Bright green on sides and top of thorax. Inner 1/2 (male) to 2/3 (female) of hindwing is yellow ↑. Yellow abdominal top spots are all triangular and of various sizes. Segment 10 with no top spots. Legs black.

Similar Species: No other snaketails are this tiny. Unmistakable.

Flight Characteristics: Undulating flight.

Hunting Technique: Males patrol over stream riffles, flying in an undulating fashion. They are most active during the middle of the day, disappearing in late afternoon and not reappearing until the late morning of the next day.

Larvae: Aquatic nymphs burrow in sandy river bottoms. They are intolerant of water conditions immediately downstream from dams.

Nature Notes:

The Pygmy Snaketail has separate western and eastern populations. Here, in its western range, it has only been found in northern Wisconsin, the western part of the U.P. and in scattered sites in eastern Minnesota. In its larger eastern range, it is found along the Eastern Seaboard and southward into Kentucky and Tennessee.

Riffle Snaketail *Ophiogomphus carolus* (male)

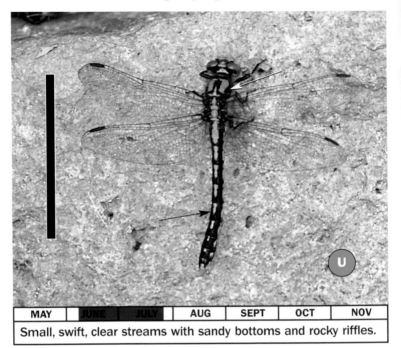

| MAY | JUNE | JULY | AUG | SEPT | OCT | NOV |

Small, swift, clear streams with sandy bottoms and rocky riffles.

Nature Notes:

The Riffle Snaketail can be very difficult to net, as it flies swiftly and very low to the water. It nearly disappears as it flies amongst the dancing sunlight of sparkling riffles.

Description: Adults average 1.7 inches long.

Adults: Boldly marked green and brown thorax ↑. Abdomen is black with crisp yellow markings. Top spots on segments 2 to 7 long and roughly triangular with notches cut out of the sides ↑. Spots on segments 8 and 9 nearly rectangular, spot on 9 is barely wider than long. Male claspers are pointed and arched but not inflated. Female resembles the male except her club is smaller. Legs are completely black.

Similar Species: Boreal Snaketail and Brook Snaketail are similar, but Boreal has a black facial stripe, and both Boreal and Brook have a triangular top spot on segment 8.

Flight Characteristics: Flies quite fast and low to the water.

Rusty Snaketail *Ophiogomphus rupinsulensis* (male)

MAY	JUNE	JULY	AUG	SEPT	OCT	NOV

Clear, cold streams and rivers.

Description: Adults average 2 inches long.

Adults: Bright green thorax with small, brown shoulder stripes and no bold side stripes, only a smaller dark, incomplete thoracic stripe. Abdomen is brownish without distinct top spots ↑; it appears rust-colored when in flight. Face and occiput are green. Yellow, lengthwise striping is evident on the legs: Males, females and juveniles are similarly marked.

Similar Species: The much larger Common Green Darner also has a bright green thorax, but the eyes are not separated.

Larvae: Aquatic nymphs are shallow burrowers in sandy creek and river bottoms. Although the Rusty Snaketail tolerates silt better than most snaketails, clear-cutting of forests can cause the nymphs to be washed away in rapid runoff or to be covered up by silt.

Nature Notes:

The snaketails have been aptly called the "trout" of the dragonfly world; they are beautiful creatures that are limited to clear, unaltered waters. Their habitat is also trout streams.

Rusty Snaketails prefer grassy, open banks for perching. Juveniles are often seen resting on grasses and in forest openings while adults alight on exposed rocks in rapids and on twigs along the river.

Wisconsin Snaketail *Ophiogomphus susbehcha* (male)

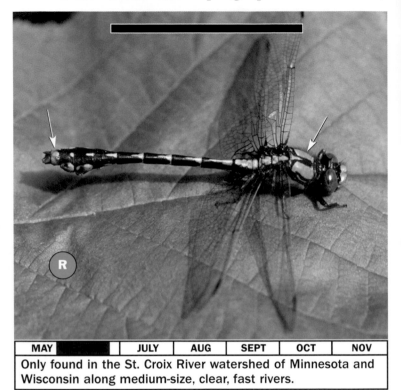

MAY		JULY	AUG	SEPT	OCT	NOV

Only found in the St. Croix River watershed of Minnesota and Wisconsin along medium-size, clear, fast rivers.

Nature Notes:

This snaketail has only recently been scientifically described and named as a species.

The range of the Wisconsin Snaketail is currently limited to the St. Croix River Watershed, which flows out of Wisconsin and along the Minnesota-Wisconsin border. Does it occur in other watersheds in the North Woods?

Aquatic nymphs burrow shallowly in sandy river bottoms.

Description: Adults average 2 inches long.

Adults: Bluish-green thorax ↑ with dark shoulder stripes and a black, rear thoracic side stripe. Face is pale yellow below and green above. Abdomen has yellow triangular top spots on segments 2 to 8 and a spot on segment 9; segment 10 is mostly yellow ↑. Female is sometimes unmarked on segments 8 and 9. Side spots on segments 8 and 9 are brownish-yellow. Eyes are gray-blue. Legs black with pale bases. The bottom set (epiproct) of male claspers are longer than the upper set (cerci).

Similar Species: Away from the St. Croix River compare closely to the Riffle, Boreal and Sand Snaketails.

The Sand Snaketail

Another new snaketail species has been found in Wisconsin. The Sand Snaketail *(Ophiogomphus* species*)* has a very limited range that just reaches into the North Woods of north central Wisconsin (it is also found in northeastern Iowa).

It is nearly identical to the Brook Snaketail *(O. aspersus)*, a New England species that is not found in our area.

Adults have a bright green thorax with a black rear thoracic stripe. Abdominal segments 2 to 10 have light yellow, triangular top spots while segments 8 and 9 have yellow side spots washed with brown. Male claspers are swollen and mostly yellow. Legs are striped with green.

As its name implies, it prefers streams and rivers with sandy bottoms. Males patrol over stream riffles without hovering. It is on the wing from late May until late July.

How many more new species are out there?

Hunting Technique: Males split their time between patrolling territories and perching on vegetation in nearby fields. The male is believed to be very short-lived.

Spiketails
Family Cordulegastridae

Spiketails are large, slender, black and yellow dragonflies whose bodies are similar to the darners. Their aqua eyes meet (or nearly meet) at a single point, as opposed to along a margin. The thorax is marked with two or three yellow side stripes. The triangles on the forewings and hindwings are of approximately equal size. The name spiketail derives from the female's long spikelike ovipositor. In Europe, they are known as "golden rings," as almost all their species show yellow markings that ring each abdomen segment.

Males fly lengthy patrols over streams seeking mates and weakly defending territories. Mated pairs will fly high up in the trees to copulate, a process that can take from one to five hours to complete. During copulation the female's exceedingly long ovipositor fits nicely into a deep slot located at the base of the male's abdomen and thorax. The female then hovers over shallow water, plunging her ovipositor into soft sediments, depositing eggs on each thrust. Abdominal segments 9 and 10, between the base of her ovipositor and the tip of the abdomen, have the ability to compress, like an accordion, each time she thrusts her ovipositor into the mud.

Spiketails are usually only locally abundant. They are secretive and not readily observed. Generally, the female keeps herself hidden away from the males until she is ready to mate.

The larvae are burrowers, but not in the same sense as the clubtails are burrowers. The spiketails burrow tail first, using their stout legs to kick away the mucky substrate while they wiggle down into the newly formed hollow. When they have settled into position, they again use their legs to move the muck over their backs. The only part of the larva visible, when so disguised, is the tops of their eyes. There they lay in wait until suitable prey happens by to trigger the awesome, toothed, grasping lip.

Four species of spiketails are found in the North Woods, all of them in the genus *Cordulegaster*. North America hosts eight species of the 33 found worldwide—the other 25 species inhabit Eurasia.

Spiketails (Genus *Cordulegaster***)**
93 Twin-spotted Spiketail
94 Arrowhead Spiketail
96 Delta-spotted Spiketail
98 Brown Spiketail

Twin-spotted Spiketail *Cordulegaster maculata* (male)

MAY	JUNE	JULY	AUG	SEPT	OCT	NOV

Clean, clear streams and small rivers in wooded areas (such as trout streams).

Description: Adults average 2.8 inches long.

Adults: A black dragonfly with pairs of bright yellow spots ↑ on its abdomen. Two bold yellow thoracic stripes. Female's ovipositor extends beyond the tip of her abdomen. Eyes are green and they touch only at one point.

Similar Species: The smaller Delta-spotted Spiketail has triangular abdominal top spots. Some female mosaic darners may have only yellow markings, but their eyes connect along a greater distance.

Hunting Technique: They search for prey in forest shadows more often than in sunlight.

Mating & Egg Laying: The female Twin-spotted oviposits alone. While hovering, she repeatedly pokes the tip of her abdomen into the bottom of a shallow stream. Males fly constant patrols just above the water's surface.

Nature Notes:

Males are commonly seen as they constantly patrol. Females are rarely spied.

The older larvae are completely developed by the time winter sets in, allowing for a very early and concentrated emergence the following spring.

Arrowhead Spiketail *Cordulegaster obliqua* (male)

MAY			AUG	SEPT	OCT	NOV

Forest seeps and tiny spring-fed streams with soft bottoms and sometimes rocks.

Nature Notes:

The handsome Arrowhead Spiketail is very wary and difficult to approach unless you can anticipate a male's patrolling run.

Female Arrowheads, like other spiketails, are secretive and hard to find.

Normally perch on grasses and twigs near the ground, but are often seen on leaves in the treetops. When disturbed, they rocket straight up and disappear above the canopy.

Description: Adults average 3.1 inches long.

Adults: Dramatic yellow arrowhead-shaped top spots on abdominal segments 3 to 7 ↑; top spot on segment 8 is rounder and on segment 9 roughly rectangular. No markings on segment 10. Female ovipositor protrudes beyond the tip of the abdomen at a length about equal to (but not longer than) segment 10. Eyes green and touching only at one point.

Similar Species: None. The arrowhead-shaped markings on the abdomen of this handsome species are distinctive.

Hunting Technique: Males fly constant patrols just above the water's surface, turning around when the water ends or they encounter an obstacle.

Spiketail eyes only contact at a single point on top of the head. This is an identifying trait of the family Cordulegastridae.

Mating & Egg Laying: The female Arrowhead oviposits alone. While hovering, she repeatedly punches the tip of her abdomen into the shallows of her little stream.

The "arrowheads" on the abdomen are striking when seen up close.

Delta-spotted Spiketail *Cordulegaster diastatops* (female)

MAY	JUNE	JULY	AUG	SEPT	OCT	NOV

Spring-fed trickles and small streams. Hunt in full sunlight.

Nature Notes:

Delta-spotteds normally perch on grasses and twigs near the ground but may also perch on leaves in the treetops.

Description: Adults average 2.4 inches long.

Adults: Our smallest spiketail. The Delta's body is black with bright yellow markings. Abdominal segments 6 to 8 have pairs of yellow triangles. Yellow on sides of female abdomen forms an almost complete stripe ↑. Black thorax is interrupted by three yellow side stripes; the middle stripe is narrowest ↑, and the rearward stripe is broadest. Face is yellow above. Although the female's ovipositor extends beyond the tip of the abdomen, it is relatively shorter than other Spiketails. Eyes are green and only very slightly separated, nearly touching at one point.

Similar Species: The larger Twin-spotted Spiketail has smaller and more evenly-sized abdominal top spots and a longer ovipositor. Some female mosaic darners also have only yellow markings, but their eyes meet along a longer margin.

Hunting Technique: Males fly constant patrols just above the water's surface, monitoring a short section of stream. The juveniles leave the water to mature as much as a mile away from their emergence site. They prefer to hunt in the full sunlight of clearings and along ditches.

Mating & Egg Laying: The female Delta-spotted oviposits alone. While hovering, she repeatedly punches the tip of her abdomen into moss above the waterline.

Brown Spiketail *Cordulegaster bilineata* (male)

MAY			AUG	SEPT	OCT	NOV

Spring-fed trickles and small streams, usually in full sunlight.

Nature Notes:

The Brown Spiketail was thought to be simply a variant of the Delta-spotted Spiketail until 1983 when it was described as a separate species.

Juveniles mature as much as a mile away from the watery habitats where they originally emerged.

Only found as far north as the northern portion of lower Michigan.

Description: Adults average 2.5 inches long.

Adults: Brown body ↑ with bright yellow markings. The two yellow thoracic stripes are equal in width. Abdominal spots are bluntly triangular ↑. Markings on segments 2 and 3 are connected. Eyes are blue-green and only slightly separated.

Similar Species: The larger Twin-spotted Spiketail has smaller and more even abdominal top spots and a longer ovipositor. Some female blue darners also have only yellow markings, but their eyes meet along a longer margin.

Hunting Technique: Males fly constant patrols just above the water's surface, monitoring a short section of stream. They hunt in clearings and along ditches, preferring full sun.

Mating & Egg Laying: While hovering, the female repeatedly pokes the tip of her abdomen into mosses just above the waterline.

Cruisers
Family Macromiidae

Cruisers are long, slender dragonflies with long legs that are armed with forked claws. On the thorax is a single side stripe. The wings are very long, stiff and slender, allowing strong, "cruising" flight. All North American species have clear wings. Their eyes are usually brilliant green and are in contact at the top of the head.

The larvae are large, flattened beasts with spidery legs and a large, pyramidal horn protruding from between the eyes. A spoon-shaped labium, or lower lip, partially covers the face. Camouflaged by a sandy bottom or silt-covered in muddier environs, the larvae lie in wait for their food to come drifting past.

During mating, the male flies his clamped female high up in the treetops for copulation. Unattended by the male, the female, who lacks a usable ovipositor, lays her eggs by washing them from her abdomen while flying at high speeds over water. She avoids streams with bedrock bottoms, preferring sand and silt substrates.

The cruisers hang vertically or obliquely on low twigs and branches when perched during the day and high up in evergreen trees overnight.

Known in Europe as the "River Emeralds," cruisers have posed a taxonomic problem for scientists for some time. They have been listed as subfamilies of both the Emerald and the Skimmer families by some authors. They are treated as a full family in this text.

There are only two cruiser species found in the North Woods and nine in North America. Over 150 species are found worldwide, mostly in the Northern Hemisphere.

Brown Cruisers (Genus *Didymops***)**
100 Stream Cruiser

River Cruisers (Genus *Macromia***)**
102 Illinois River Cruiser

Stream Cruiser *Didymops transversa* (male)

MAY	JUNE	JULY	AUG	SEPT	OCT	NOV

Small sandy-bottomed forest streams, preferably without much weed growth. Also larger lakes with wave-swept shores.

Nature Notes:

The swift-flying, dull-colored Stream Cruiser perches obliquely on twigs or hangs vertically from stems or leaves.

The genus *Didymops* is known only from North America and contains but two species, the other being *D. floridensis* known only from Florida and adjacent states.

While camping on an island of the Whiteface Reservoir in northeastern Minnesota, I found a Stream Cruiser emerging while it was perched on the roof of my tent, which was set up a considerable distance from the lakeshore.

Description: Adults average 2.2 inches long.

Adults: Dull brown body with a single yellow thoracic side stripe ↑. Broad, yellow stripe across the face is quite visible ↑. The pale yellow abdominal top spots fade with age. Leading wing vein is brown when mature. Male claspers are yellow, and his abdomen is noticeably clubbed ↑. Eyes green at maturity.

Juveniles: Brown eyes. Female's eyes take longer to turn green than the male's. Yellow areas of abdomen are brighter and more defined, dulling with maturity.

Similar Species: The much larger Illinois River Cruiser also has only one thoracic stripe, but it is black instead of brown.

Hunting Technique: The Stream Cruiser flies low when hunting, dodging in and out of tight spaces between plants.

The broad, yellow stripe across the face is a good mark to look for in the field.

Mating & Egg Laying: Mating and egg laying can occur even before mature eye color is attained. Males patrol regular beats as long as 100 yards along shorelines. The female rapidly dips the tip of her abdomen into the water when ovipositing.

Larvae: The larva of the Stream Cruiser is striking with its spidery, long legs and broadly flattened abdomen. They inhabit well-aerated, sandy shallows of lakes and smaller streams. The exuviae may be found quite a distance from the water's edge and as much as five feet off the ground on a tree trunk.

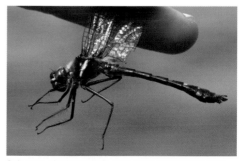

Spines on the legs aid in capturing and holding prey before the victims are transferred to the mouth.

Illinois River Cruiser *Macromia illinoiensis* (male)

MAY	JUNE			SEPT	OCT	NOV

Larger streams to large rivers. Large lakes, especially in areas with exposed shoreline.

Nature Notes:

When at rest, they hang vertically from the end of a twig.

Description: Adults average 2.8 inches long.

Adults: Body is nearly black with a slight metallic luster and a single yellow thoracic side stripe ↑. Sparsely marked with bright yellow on abdomen. The large, yellow spot on segment 7 ↑ is visible during flight. Pale abdominal segments 7 to 10 are swollen to form a club. Female has no club. Similar in size to the mosaic darners. Bright green eyes.

Similar Species: The Stream Cruiser has a lighter brown body and more yellow abdominal markings than the Illinois River Cruiser.

Flight Characteristics: During warmer weather, they fly erratically, alternating between bursts of speed and sustained soars.

Hunting Technique: The Illinois River Cruiser is, indeed, a famed cruiser. It patrols long, linear stretches of fifty yards or more,

Though called the "Illinois River Cruiser," this species ranges from eastern Manitoba to Nova Scotia and south to central Florida and Texas.

attaining long-distance cruising speeds to rival those of any other dragonfly.

Mating & Egg Laying: Mating takes place while the pair is perched in a tree.

River cruisers have posed a taxonomic problem for some time. They have been considered subfamilies of both the Emerald and the Skimmer families. In this book we treat them as a separate family.

Emeralds
Family Corduliidae

The bright green eyes of most emeralds look, indeed, like glowing jewels. Eyes contact one another on top of the head. These small to medium-size slender dragonflies are usually dark in color, the thorax hinting of a green metallic luster. The forewing and hindwing triangles are different sizes and the club-shaped anal loop of the hindwing is long, has a midrib and has little or no "toe."

Female emeralds do not have ovipositors, but many do have an egg-laying spout that aids in depositing eggs in mud. Males hover often while on patrol.

Some emerald larvae are sprawlers and some are crawlers. The sprawlers spend their time awaiting prey amongst the bottom detritus. Their hairy bodies attract silt and sediment to aid in camouflage. Crawlers are less hairy and patterned with green and brown. They spend their time pursuing prey in the greenery of their aquatic world.

Native to the bogs and muskegs of the North, the emeralds may be only locally common at best. Many are secretive creatures. Although not the showiest of dragonflies, their rarity and the remoteness of their haunts have created a cult following among some serious dragonfly enthusiasts.

Twenty two of North America's 49 species inhabit the North Woods. The Corduliidae is primarily a Northern Hemisphere family with over 200 species worldwide.

The Baskettails — Genus *Tetragoneuria*

The members of the genus *Tetragoneuria* are known collectively as the baskettails. The female carries her blob of eggs on the lower side of her abdomen. (You might say all her eggs are in one basket!) This ball, or "basket," of eggs will be attached to a submerged plant. The mass of between 500 and 1,000 eggs unravels underwater into a single strand six inches long.

Baskettails are relatively drab with brown bodies and no metallic luster. Brown or green eyes, though less intensely green than in other emeralds.

The genera *Tetragoneuria* (Common, Spiny and Beaverpond Baskettails) and *Epicordulia* (Prince Baskettail) were recently split from the genus *Epitheca*. If you are lucky enough to observe all four of these species, it will soon become apparent that the Prince is, indeed, quite different from the rest of our baskettails.

The Striped Emeralds — Genus *Somatochlora*

Grouped together as the "striped emeralds," the *Somatochlora* are known for their metallic green thoraxes that are marked with yellow spots and stripes. There is often a yellow spot on the side of abdominal segment 2, which makes it look as if the thorax has three spots or stripes. *Somatochlora* species are best differentiated by their diagnostic abdominal appendages. Male claspers are distinctive and the female ovipositors are, in most species, spout-like. The hindwing triangle has an extra vein that creates two triangles.

The larvae are crawlers that clamber over and through the mix of decaying vegetation in their habitats.

Adult striped emeralds feed in mixed species swarms, sometimes even with blue darners (genus *Aeshna*). The mass of emeralds can reach from the ground up to the treetops as they gorge on small insects.

Common Emeralds (Genus *Cordulia***)**
  106 American Emerald

Little Emeralds (Genus *Dorocordulia***)**
  108 Racket-tailed Emerald

Boghaunters (Genus *Williamsonia***)**
  109 Ebony Boghaunter

Baskettails (Genus *Tetragoneuria* — **formerly** *Epitheca***)**
  110 Common Baskettail
  112 Spiny Baskettail
  114 Beaverpond Baskettail

Prince Baskettail (Genus *Epicordulia* — **formerly** *Epitheca***)**
  115 Prince Baskettail

Striped Emeralds (Genus *Somatochlora***)**
  116 Brush-tipped Emerald
  118 Clamp-tipped Emerald
  120 Delicate Emerald
  121 Forcipate Emerald
  122 Hine's Emerald
  123 Hudsonian Emerald
  124 Incurvate Emerald
  125 Kennedy's Emerald
  126 Lake Emerald
  127 Ocellated Emerald
  128 Plains Emerald
  129 Ringed Emerald
  130 Ski-tailed Emerald
  132 Williamson's Emerald

Shadowdragons (Genus *Neurocordulia***)**
  134 Stygian Shadowdragon

American Emerald *Cordulia shurtleffii* (male)

| MAY | JUNE | JULY | AUG | SEPT | OCT | NOV |

Bog ponds and boggy lakes. Also forest ponds, small lakes, fens and sedge marshes.

Nature Notes:

The American Emerald is often the most common emerald in its range. Look for the "dart and hover, dart and hover" behavior as the males patrol their shifting territories along the boggy edges of small lakes and ponds.

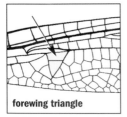

forewing triangle

Description: Adults average 1.9 inches long.

Adults: The metallic-green and brown thorax is very hairy ↑ with no yellow side stripes. Abdomen is black and narrow to segment 3, widens to segment 8, then narrowing in segments 9 and 10. Between segments 2 and 3 there is a narrow, yellow ring around the abdomen. Lower male appendages are broadly forked ↑. Female abdomen is more cylindrical. Eyes are brilliant green. Cross-vein in forewing triangle ↑.

Similar Species: The Racket-tailed Emerald is noticeably shorter and smaller than the American. Also, compare the wing venation. The "striped emeralds" (genus *Somatochlora*) usually have yellow thoracic side stripes and their abdominal appendages are larger than the

Amber wing patches are small but visible. Also note the yellow ring around the base of the abdomen.

American's. Also, other male striped emeralds have claspers that are straight or turned in rather than conspicuously turned out, as in the American.

Hunting Technique: American Emeralds have been observed feeding on smaller flying insects as well as preying on relatively defenseless and weak teneral (newly emerged) damselflies and dragonflies.

Mating & Egg Laying: The female taps the water's surface with her abdomen when laying eggs, often among sedges and other emergent vegetation.

Larvae: The larvae are known to feed heavily on amphipods (scuds) and on the larvae of midges.

Racket-tailed Emerald *Dorocordulia libera* (male)

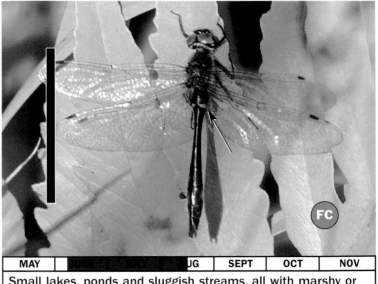

| MAY | JUNE JULY AUG | SEPT | OCT | NOV |

Small lakes, ponds and sluggish streams, all with marshy or boggy edges and acidic water.

Nature Notes:

The genus *Dorocordulia*, or the "little emeralds" is strictly North American and is represented by only two species.

Juveniles frequent wooded paths, traveling some distance before they turn around.

They usually fly about four feet above the water.

forewing triangle

Description: Adults average 1.6 inches long.

Adults: The expanded abdominal club (segments 7 to 9), is especially large in the male. Abdominal segment 3 is ringed with an uneven, yellowish band ↑. The thorax is completely metallic green and bronze with no side stripes. No cross-vein in forewing triangle ↑.

Similar Species: The Racket-tailed Emerald is not a clubtail, despite its expanded abdomen. The eyes are in contact with one another, unlike clubtails. Compare the forewing triangles of the Racket-tailed to the American Emerald. The Racket-tailed is not as likely to follow the shoreline, preferring to wander freely over the water. Also they fly at a higher level than the American, not patrolling a regular beat.

Larvae: The larvae are fond of overhanging, boggy edges and may be found living below them. Exuviae are rarely found more than a foot above the water's surface.

Ebony Boghaunter *Williamsonia fletcheri* (male)

MAY	JUNE	JULY	AUG	SEPT	OCT	NOV

Boggy pools surrounded by forest.

Description: Adults average 1.3 inches long.

Adults: The entire body is very dark brown or black but not metallic like other emeralds. Only the face is metallic green. The male has two light rings on the rearward margins of segments 2 and 3 ↑. Females have three rings on segments 2 to 4.

Similar Species: The whitefaces (genus *Leucorrhinia*) are similar in size, but all have the characteristic white face. The Black Meadowhawk flies much later in the summer. The Ringed Boghaunter is not considered a North Woods species, but it is found in central Wisconsin and, with further exploration, it may be found in our range. It is similar in size to the Ebony, but has an orange face and orange rings around each abdominal segment.

Flight Characteristics: The boghaunters are weak fliers.

Nature Notes:

The aquatic nymph, of this species was not discovered until the early 1990s.

Boghaunters are easily viewed as they perch low in sunny forest openings.

The Boghaunters are glacial relicts—a remnant population from the Ice Age of 10,000 years ago.

Populations tend to be very small and, therefore, are very susceptible to local extinction.

The Ebony's range surrounds the northern portions of the Great Lakes, barely reaching Minnesota and southeast Manitoba.

Common Baskettail *Tetragoneuria cynosura* (female)

MAY		LY	AUG	SEPT	OCT	NOV

Marsh-edged lakes and bays, slow stream outlets, usually acidic water environments with mucky bottoms.

Nature Notes:

Common Baskettails will congregate over swarms of suitable prey.

Formerly placed in the genus *Epitheca*

Male claspers in profile. Note the "step" on the cerci.

Description: Adults average 1.6 inches long.

Adults: The dark brown abdomen has a series of yellow-orange spots along the sides. Forehead has a black T-spot that can be partial or absent. Male abdominal appendages are diagnostic ↑. Female appendages are short and farther apart than other baskettails ↑. Hindwings usually have a triangular patch at the base ↑. Wings sometimes clear. Eyes range from blue to green to reddish-brown.

Similar Species: Spiny and Beaverpond Baskettails have clear wings. Clear-winged Commons are rare but must be differentiated by comparing abdominal appendages.

Flight Characteristics: The flight of feeding Common Baskettails is worth checking out; they fly in loopy patterns with swift vertical maneuvers. One biologist called them "ace stunt flyers."

Thankfully, 90 percent of our northern Common Baskettails show the diagnostic hindwing patches. On the ten percent that don't show them, one must compare abdominal appendages to separate from Beaverpond and Spiny Baskettails.

Hunting Technique: Adults usually feed away from water at a height of over six feet.

Mating & Egg Laying: Males patrol shoreline beats ten to thirty feet long. Males will hover for several minutes over suitable egg laying sites. Although he may feed occasionally while defending his territory, it is only a secondary activity. Both sexes fly slowly, about three feet above the water, when looking for a mate. During this flight, they do not hover but fly long straight lines.

Larvae: Aquatic nymphs emerge while perched on slender reeds or rushes. Often several exuviae may be found on a single stem.

Spiny Baskettail *Tetragoneuria spinigera* (female)

MAY	JUNE	JULY	AUG	SEPT	OCT	NOV

Marshy edges of small to medium lakes and slow streams; they are almost always in acidic water environments.

Nature Notes:

Spiny Baskettails are often found together in swarms of dozens, or even hundreds, and often far from water.

Spiny Baskettails emerge about a week and a half after Beaverpond Baskettails.

Formerly placed in the genus *Epitheca*

Male claspers in profile. Note the downpointing "tooth."

Description: Adults average 1.9 inches long.

Adults: Dark brown abdomen has a series of yellow-orange spots along the sides. Forehead has a black T-spot. Male abdominal appendages have a downward pointing tooth visible in profile ↑. Female appendages are long ↑ (as long as segments 9 and 10) and close together. The male's eyes are blue and the female's eyes are green.

Similar Species: The Spiny, the Beaverpond and the Common Baskettails are all very similar. Differentiate between them by comparing the abdominal appendages.

Just barely visible in this male's terminal claspers is the downward pointing tooth that separates this species from Beaverponds and Commons without wing patches. Also note the male's iridescent blue-green eyes.

Spiny Baskettails may gather in large concentrations, especially after mass emergences in the spring and early summer. Thousands may emerge in just a few hours.

Beaverpond Baskettail *Tetragoneuria canis* (male)

| | | LY | AUG | SEPT | OCT | NOV |

Boggy ponds, lakes and streams. Acidic waters with low organic content.

Nature Notes:

The Beaverpond Baskettails seldom rest when actively hunting and are commonly found in swarms.

Females display their darkened wings in flight.

Formerly placed in the genus *Epitheca*.

Male claspers in profile. Note the projecting bumps.

Description: Adults average 1.8 inches long.

Adults: Dark brown abdomen has a series of yellow-orange spots along the sides. Forehead has no black T-spot ↑. Male claspers show a downpointing bump↑ and an upper spur ↑ in profile. Female append -ages are broad, closely spaced and shorter than segments 9 and 10. Female hindwing patches may extend to stigma on mature individual. Eyes range from blue to metallic green.

Similar Species: Spiny, Beaverpond and Common Baskettails are all very similar. Differentiate between them by comparing abdominal appendages. The Beaverpond is the only baskettail which never has a T-spot on the forehead, although occasionally the Common lacks a T-spot as well.

Hunting Technique: They seldom rest when hunting and are commonly found in swarms.

Prince Baskettail *Epicordulia princeps* (male)

MAY	JUNE	JULY	AUG	SEPT	OCT	NOV

Larger lakes and ponds. Slower, large to medium-size rivers.

Description: Average 2.2 to 3.2 inches long.

Adults: Wings have large dark patches at the base, middle and tips ↑. Wing markings occasionally very reduced. Abdomen is about as long as the hindwing and is slender, being widest at segment 6.

Similar Species: Large size and bold wing patches make the Prince distinct among baskettails. The Lake Emerald has a similar abdomen but no dark wing patches.

Hunting Technique: Mature adults feed on large, high-flying mayflies.

Nature Notes:

The Prince Baskettail is our largest species of emerald.

In good weather a mature adult may fly almost continuously from dawn to dusk, rarely stopping to perch.

Formerly placed in the genus *Epitheca*.

Brush-tipped Emerald *Somatochlora walshii* (female)

| MAY | JUNE | JULY | AUG | SEPT | OCT | NOV |

Slow, clear streams that course through boggy or marshy habitat, usually in the presence of conifers.

Nature Notes:

Emeralds are named for their brilliant green eyes and metallic green thoraxes.

Description: Adults average 1.9 inches long.

Adults: Male's abdomen is short, only as long as a wing. The metallic green thorax shows two well-defined, unequal yellow stripes ↑. Small, yellowish abdominal side spots at joints between segments 5 to 7. Male abdominal appendages are blunt and uniquely hairy ↑ (hence the name, "Brush-tipped"). Female abdominal appendages are very long and the ovipositor is diagonally positioned relative to the abdomen.

Similar Species: The Ocellated Emerald has oval thoracic side spots, no abdominal side spots and the abdominal appendages in both sexes are very different from the Brush-tipped.

Brush-tipped Emeralds are quite colorful with their copper and green sheen, yellow stripes, bright green eyes and multi-colored face.

Hunting Technique: Flies swiftly along the edges of coniferous stands and over marshes. Flight can last into dusk.

Mating & Egg Laying: Males pause often to hover during their patrolling runs. To lay eggs, the female repeatedly dips her abdomen amongst reeds and rushes growing in very slowly flowing water.

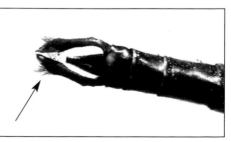

The whiskered tips of the male Brush-tipped's abdominal appendages are unlike those of any other North American species.

Clamp-tipped Emerald *Somatochlora tenebrosa* (male)

| MAY | JUNE | JULY | AUG | SEPT | OCT | NOV |

Small, shaded forest streams with slow, perhaps swampy, sections separated by small riffles.

Nature Notes:

The shade-loving Clamp-tipped is an aggressive flyer and may be difficult to catch.

Description: Adults average 2.3 inches long.

Adults: The thorax is a metallic dark brown with green highlights and two yellow side spots that fade after maturity. The upper lip is usually orange. Wing veins and stigma are brown. Abdomen is dark with only a few faint side spots. Male's claspers are dramatic with a broad circular opening between the upper and lower components ↑. Female appendages are thin and longer than segments 9 and 10. Ovipositor is slender, pointed downward and longer than segment 9 ↑. Female's wings become tea-stained with age.

Female Clamp-tippeds have a long ovipositor that slants backwards at an angle. Her abdominal appendages are actually longer than segments 9 and 10 combined.

Similar Species: The male Hine's Emerald also has dramatic claspers, but they show a more oval opening in profile. Hine's also show bright yellow side spots on the thorax. The female Williamson's Emerald is nearly identical, but her wings are light-amber instead of tea-stained, and she has pale abdominal side spots on segments 4 to 8. The female Ocellated Emerald has a similarly-shaped ovipositor, but is a much smaller dragonfly.

Hunting Technique: The Clamp-tipped hunts in shaded areas along forest borders and over water. May hunt until after sunset.

Mating & Egg Laying: Females lay eggs while hovering near rocks or plants. They also place eggs into mud at the edge of streams.

Delicate Emerald *Somatochlora franklini* (male)

MAY	JUNE	JULY	AUG	SEPT	OCT	NOV

Spring-fed, mossy fens. Shallow flows dominated by dense stands of sedges or horsetails.

Nature Notes:

The Delicate Emerald will fly with other spotted emeralds in mixed-species swarms, feeding from the ground to above the treetops.

Female lays eggs in wet moss with her abdomen beneath her at an angle just forward of vertical.

Description: Adults average 2 inches long.

Adults: A very slender and short-winged dragonfly with a small basal brown spot on the hindwings. Abdomen thin ↑. Female wings may be tea-stained. Forward thoracic side stripe is pale or missing. Male's abdomen is fifty percent longer than a wing and has small, yellow side spots. Female's ovipositor is yellow, horizontal and as long as segment 9.

Similar Species: The Delicate Emerald is the only species with all of the following attributes combined: upper face black, one pale thoracic side stripe (or none), basal brown spot on short hindwings and a long abdomen with few side markings.

Forcipate Emerald *Somatochlora forcipata* (female)

MAY	JUNE	JULY	AUG	SEPT	OCT	NOV

Small, slow, spring-fed streams that wind through boggy areas and alder swamps.

Description: Adults average 2 inches long.

Adults: Two oval-shaped, similar-sized yellow side spots on thorax ↑. Small, yellow spots on sides of abdominal segments 5 to 8 of male and 3 to 7 of female. Female's ovipositor is mostly yellow and parallel to the abdomen and is longer than abdominal segment 9. Female abdominal appendages are longer than abdominal segments 9 and 10 together. Male's clasper is arched in profile ↑.

Similar Species: The Delicate Emerald and Kennedy's Emerald are differentiated by comparing the shapes of the male claspers and the positions of the female ovipositors.

Mating & Egg Laying: The female lays eggs by tapping her abdomen in the water at irregular intervals.

Nature Notes:

Forcipate Emeralds are found flying along shaded trails, roadways, and in forest openings, especially in spruce stands.

Hine's Emerald *Somatochlora hineana* (male)

MAY	JUNE			SEPT	OCT	NOV

Found along seepages over limestone bedrock. Also seasonally dry fens and marshes. West shore of Lake Michigan only.

Nature Notes:

Very rare and local. Only found in the right habitat along Lake Michigan in the U.P. and Northeast Wisconsin. Federally endangered.

The end of the female's abdomen becomes muddy from laying eggs in waterlogged clay. The light-colored, dry mud contrasts with the darker color of the rest of the dragonfly, giving her a unique appearance in flight.

The aquatic larvae have adapted to endure periodic drought conditions and may overwinter in the burrowed tunnels of crayfish.

Description: Adults average 2.4 inches long.

Adults: Two yellow stripes on a metallic-green thorax ↑; the rear stripe is more squat. Third yellow stripe on the side of abdomen segment 1. Face is mostly yellow. Dark abdomen with an interrupted thin ring around segment 2. Most females have tea-stained wings. Male claspers show a broad oval opening in silhouette ↑. Female abdominal appendages are longer than 9 and 10. Ovipositor is longer than segment 9 and nearly horizontal.

Similar Species: The male Clamp-tipped Emerald's claspers have a circular opening in profile, and the female's ovipositor is perpendicular.

Hunting Technique: The Hine's Emerald is an early riser, feeding as early as 7a.m. on warm days, but is most active late in the morning. They may also group with other species in the afternoon or evening to feed en masse.

Hudsonian Emerald *Somatochlora hudsonica* (male)

MAY	JU	JULY	AUG	SEPT	OCT	NOV

Ponds, lakes and very slow streams. Prefers boggy environs with little water movement.

Description: Adults average 2.1 inches long.

Adults: Only the forward, pale-yellow thoracic spot is visible on the metallic brownish-green thorax. Abdomen is accented by narrow, whitish rings around the junctions of all of the segments ↑. Male claspers are a little hairy but bare at the tips. Female appendages are slightly longer than segments 9 and 10. Her ovipositor is $2/3$ the length of segment 9.

Similar Species: Female Ringed and Lake Emeralds do not have a visible ovipositor. The nearly identical male Ringed has pale spots on segment 10 adjacent to the claspers and is duller on segments 2 to 4. The Lake has a browner thorax with no obvious thoracic stripes and will fly over expanses of open water, whereas the Hudsonian and the Ringed stay close to shore. The Hudsonian is smaller than the Lake but larger than the Ringed.

Nature Notes:

In our area, only found north of Lake Superior in Ontario. But watch for it near bogs south of the border.

Hudsonian and Ringed Emeralds prefer the same habitats and are often found together. They are very similar in appearance and care must be taken in their identification.

The female taps her abdomen repeatedly on the water's surface during oviposition. Males patrol about a foot above the water near the bank.

Incurvate Emerald *Somatochlora incurvata* (male)

MAY	JUNE	JULY	AUG	SEPT	OCT	NOV

Large, open sedge meadows. Sometimes in bog pools.

Nature Notes:

Males can be very aggressive in securing females and chasing off other male striped emeralds, as well as the large male *Aeshna* darners that venture into their territories. At other times, they show no territoriality towards other males.

They patrol bog ponds, hovering often.

The female lays eggs by dipping her abdomen into the water at regular intervals.

Description: Adults average 2.4 inches long.

Adults: Metallic green thorax with pale and indefinite side spots ↑. Face is dark. Male's abdomen is 1/3 longer than the length of his wing. Indistinct abdominal side spots present from segments 4 or 5 to 7 or 8 ↑. Female's yellowish ovipositor is long, reaching just short of the end of segment 10. Her appendages are barely longer than segments 9 and 10.

Similar Species: The Forcipate Emerald is smaller, has definite oval thoracic side spots and the claspers and ovipositor are shaped differently.

Hunting Technique: Incurvate Emeralds will join hunting swarms with other species of emeralds, feeding until, or after, sundown while the temperature is still warm.

Kennedy's Emerald *Somatochlora kennedyi* (male)

| MAY | JUNE | JULY | AUG | SEPT | OCT | NOV |

Slow streams through open areas. Also cold bog ponds.

Description: Adults average 2.1 inches long.

Adults: Only the forward, pale yellow thoracic spot is visible on the metallic green thorax ↑. Abdomen is long and slender (1/4 to 1/3 longer than any of the wings). Face is covered with a dense mat of short hairs. Wings mostly clear with a faint yellowish-smoky tint toward the bases. Female's ovipositor is mostly yellow and lies parallel to the abdomen; it is equal in length to abdominal segment 9. Female's abdominal appendages are as long or longer than abdominal segments 9 and 10 together.

Similar Species: The Delicate and Forcipate Emeralds are both closely related to the Kennedy's but are easily differentiated by comparing the shapes of the male claspers and the positions of the female ovipositors.

Hunting Technique: Hunts along shaded trails, roadways and streams.

Nature Notes:

The Kennedy's Emerald is a fairly shy species.

It is often encountered with others in the "Kennedy clan" on hilltops far from water.

Female lays eggs by tapping her abdomen in the water amidst emergent vegetation at irregular intervals of three to five seconds.

Lake Emerald *Somatochlora cingulata* (male)

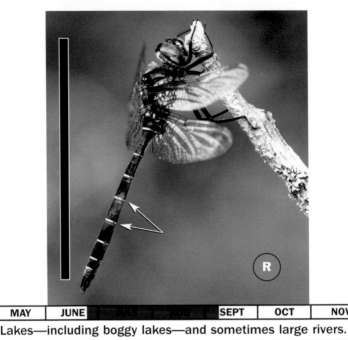

MAY	JUNE		SEPT	OCT	NOV

Lakes—including boggy lakes—and sometimes large rivers.

Nature Notes:

A very boreal dragonfly whose range extends into far northern Labrador. The southern edge of its range just dips into the North Woods.

Males fly far out over large lakes, never hovering and rarely coming to shore.

Description: Adults average 2.5 inches long.

Adults: Male's abdomen is long with pale rings between all segments ↑. Thorax is brown, stocky and unmarked. Wings are tinted brown, darkening with age. Female has no ovipositor and her abdominal appendages are quite a bit longer than segments 9 and 10.

Similar Species: Other similar striped emeralds have thoracic markings. The larger Prince Baskettail has similar body markings but the wings have large dark patches.

Flight Characteristics: Extremely fast flyers. They fly an unpredictable beat and never seem to hover.

Mating & Egg Laying: The female taps her abdomen repeatedly on the water's surface during egg laying. This is usually done near a lake outlet but not in the outgoing stream. Males seem not to be territorial.

Ocellated Emerald *Somatochlora minor* (female)

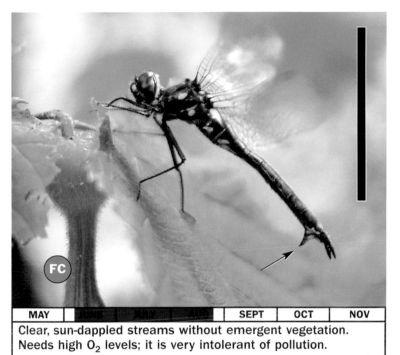

| MAY | | | | SEPT | OCT | NOV |

Clear, sun-dappled streams without emergent vegetation.
Needs high O$_2$ levels; it is very intolerant of pollution.

Description: Adults average 1.8 inches long.

Adults: Male's abdomen is short, about as long as a wing. Two yellow, oval spots on the dark metallic-green thorax ↑. Male abdominal appendages turn slightly inwards, the tips sometimes cross each other ↑. Female abdominal appendages are quite long, and the ovipositor is very large, yellowish and perpendicular to abdomen ↑.

Similar Species: The Brush-tipped Emerald has thoracic side stripes instead of ovals, abdominal side spots on segments 5 to 7 and very different abdominal appendages.

Flight Characteristics: Males fly quickly, stopping to hover for as long as half a minute during patrolling runs.

Hunting Technique: Prefers to feed along wooded edges and in sunlit clearings.

Nature Notes:

Ranges across all of subarctic Canada and south into the North Woods and northern Rocky Mountains.

Plains Emerald   *Somatochlora ensigera* (male)

| MAY | JUNE | JULY | AUG | SEPT | OCT | NOV |

Small streams in plains or woodlands.

Description: Adults average 2 inches long.

Adults: On the thorax are two bright yellow side stripes outlined in black ↑; a third yellow spot is evident on the side of abdominal segment 2. Face is mostly yellow. Abdomen is dark ↑ but for faint rings at segments 8 to 10. Female has broad yellow side spots on segments 2 to 6. Her appendages are shorter than segments 9 and 10, and the slender ovipositor is about as long as segment 8. Wings have a spray of yellow at the bases and brown veins. Claspers are not sharply bent at tips.

Similar Species: The rare Hine's Emerald is larger, and both sexes have quite different abdominal appendages. Other similar species do not have yellow faces.

Hunting Technique: They hawk insects at a height of twenty to thirty feet but are seldom seen far from their breeding waters.

Nature Notes:

Plains Emeralds perch on overhanging stems above streams.

Female oviposits just above waterline in clay banks and along gravel bars exposed by the lower water levels of mid summer. She may also drop eggs into shallow water beneath a canopy of overhanging grasses. Males patrol along stream banks until late in the day.

Ringed Emerald *Somatochlora albicincta* (male)

MAY	JUNE	JULY	AUG	SEPT	OCT	NOV

Ponds, lakes and very slow streams. Prefers boggy habitats with little water movement.

Description: Adults average 1.9 inches long.

Adults: The front pale-yellow stripe is most visible on the metallic bronzy-green thorax ↑. Narrow whitish rings around all abdomen segments ↑. Male's abdomen has pale spots on segment 10 immediately adjacent to the claspers. His claspers are slightly hairy but bare at the tips. Female appendages are slightly longer than segments 9 and 10, and she lacks an ovipositor.

Similar Species: Both the Hudsonian and Lake Emeralds show pale abdominal rings; but the Lake has no thoracic spots, and the larger Hudsonian has brighter thoracic spots.

Mating & Egg Laying: The female taps her abdomen repeatedly on the water's surface to lay eggs. Males patrol weedy shorelines, inspecting every nook and cranny.

Nature Notes:

In our area, only found north of Lake Superior in Ontario. But keep your eyes open!

The Ringed Emerald is very aggressive and will attack and drive away species much larger than itself (like the Canada Darner).

Rarely found far from its breeding waters.

Ringed Emeralds shun open water, preferring to stay close to shore.

Ski-tailed Emerald *Somatochlora elongata* (male)

MAY	JUNE			SEPT	OCT	NOV

Slow streams with intermittent rapids. Lake inlets or outlets.

Nature Notes:

In addition to resembling the Ocellated Emerald, the Ski-tailed is also often found in the same waters as the Ocellated.

Description: Adults average 2.3 inches long.

Adults: Two bright yellow thoracic side stripes, the first being longer, the second is more oval. Yellow blob on segment 2 as well ↑. Sides of the thorax are green, bronzy in the front. Abdomen is black beyond segment 3. Male claspers are ski-shaped. Female ovipositor is wide and triangular in side view ↑. Female abdominal appendages are blunt and are about as long as segments 9 and 10.

Similar Species: The Ocellated Emerald is significantly smaller. Other similar species have

It is hard to miss the female's large triangular ovipositor. Also note her long, blunt cerci. They are about as long as segments 9 and 10 combined.

one or more of the following attributes that differ from the Ski-tailed: yellow side spots on much of the abdomen, narrow ovipositor (female) or a different clasper shape (male).

Mating & Egg Laying: To deposit eggs, the female strikes her abdomen on the shore then on the water, back and forth repeatedly in a random rhythm. The dips in the water are apparently intended to clean mud and debris from the female's egg laying parts. Males patrol regular beats along the shoreline, about one to two feet above the water.

Williamson's Emerald *Somatochlora williamsoni* (male)

FC

| MAY | JUNE | JULY | AUG | SEPT | OCT | NOV |

Slow streams and clear lakes; sometimes found in bog ponds.

Nature Notes:

Williamson's avoid direct sunlight. They hunt and patrol over shaded water.

Williamson's Emerald nymphs do not compete well with the nymphs of skimmers and are therefore less likely to inhabit boggy ponds and more likely in small, shaded streams with undercut banks.

Description: Adults average 2.3 inches long.

Adults: Dark metallic green thorax shows pale yellow thoracic spots ↑. Small, pale side spots on sides of abdomen. Abdomen longer than the wings. Male claspers have a slight inward curve. Female ovipositor is perpendicular to the abdomen and longer than abdominal segment 9. Her abdominal appendages are longer than abdominal segments 9 and 10 together. Female's wings may be yellowish.

Similar Species: Kennedy's Emerald only has one thoracic side spot and the female's ovipositor is parallel to the abdomen. The Clamp-tipped Emerald male has diagnostic

Dried mud on the tip of a female's abdomen is easily visible in flight. Her abdomen gets caked as she deposits her eggs in muddy shorelines.

abdominal appendages, but the female is very similar to the Williamson's. The Clamp-tipped usually has clear wings as opposed to the often yellowish wings of the Williamson's.

Hunting Technique: They hunt and patrol over shaded water but will fly higher when the lake or pond is in the sunlight. Commonly seen hawking insects among the treetops along wooded edges.

Mating & Egg Laying: The shy female lays eggs by tapping her ovipositor on the mud just above the waterline before darting back into the woods.

Stygian Shadowdragon *Neurocordulia yamaskanensis*

MAY	JU			AUG	SEPT	OCT	NOV

Shorelines of large lakes and rivers where there is much wave action. Also near splashing water from waterfalls or rapids.

Nature Notes:

The word "Stygian" refers to the utter darkness of Hell's River Styx, and describes the shadowdragon's ability to hunt after dark.

Some dragonfly enthusiasts seem to have a sixth sense about Stygians ("Use the Force, Luke") and can pick them out of darkness as if it were daylight.

Description: Adults average 2 inches long.

Adult: Overall brown. Abdominal segments 4 to 8 have orange-yellow spots along the sides ↑. The base of the hindwings have a region of bold, darkened venation with an amber fill ↑.

Similar Species: None of our other dragonflies show the same wing venation pattern with amber coloration as the Stygian Shadowdragon.

Hunting Technique: The Stygian Shadow dragon is primarily active during late dusk and on into moonlit evenings, chalking up perhaps only thirty minutes of air time each day.

Stygian flight coincides with the evening, mass flights of certain mayflies, on whom they feed. Heavy overcast days may be dark enough for Stygians to initiate hunting flights.

Mating & Egg Laying: The males may be observed (if it's light enough to see) flying low to the water along the shore, whereas the females often fly higher. A male will shoot upwards, grab a female and fly off to the tree-tops where mating will occur.

Larvae: Stygian nymphs have been found below waterfalls in water ten feet deep. Also found in shallows where sufficient oxygen exists.

Skimmers
Family Libellulidae

The ubiquitous skimmers are the quintessential pond-dwelling dragonflies of illustrations and childhood memory. They range from small to large and are often stout. Eyes contact at the top of the head. The hindwing is rounded at the base and many species have patches of color on their wings. The forewing and hindwing triangles are different sizes.

Skimmer mating takes place, in almost all cases, while in flight. The female skimmer has a non-functional ovipositor. She is usually guarded by the male during egg laying.

Most skimmers are horizontal or oblique perchers seen on twigs, grasses or on the ground. In fact, in Europe the Libellulidae is known as the Percher family.

Libellulidae is the largest dragonfly family in North America. We find about 28 different skimmer species in the North Woods, 103 species in North America and more than 1,000 species worldwide.

The Meadowhawks — Genus *Sympetrum*

Members of the genus *Sympetrum*—the meadowhawks—are familiar denizens of grassy meadows, marshes and lakeshores. They are readily approached (except for the Variegated Meadowhawk) and are easily photographed. In most species the mature males are red. Most are summer species that fly into autumn and a few can even be found in November!

Some meadowhawk species are so similar (especially the females and the juveniles) that they are practically indistinguishable. This can be frustrating, but my advice is to learn how to shrug and simply call it a *Sympetrum* or a "red meadowhawk." This can be difficult but it prevents misidentifications and ulcers. There are a few characteristics that can help identify ambiguous species, but they usually involve a microscope and a book that is about three inches thick.

The Whitefaces — Genus *Leucorrhinia*

The small skimmers known as whitefaces, not surprisingly, have white faces, dark bodies, black legs and small, basal black spots on the wings. Body markings range from red to yellow and pruinosity is expected in mature individuals of some species. Several whitefaces are so similar that they are difficult to identify—especially the juveniles.

Mating takes place while the pair is perched near the water's edge and lasts for three to twenty minutes. Males usually hover guard the female during egg laying. Occasionally a male will clasp a competing male as he would a prospective mate and hold him until his mate is finished laying her eggs. This is called "karate guarding."

The larvae are well-camouflaged crawlers, hunting amongst the green vegetation of still or slowly flowing waters.

King Skimmers (Genus *Libellula*)
138 Four-spotted Skimmer
140 Slaty Skimmer
142 Twelve-spotted Skimmer
144 Common Whitetail
146 Widow Skimmer
148 Chalk-fronted Corporal

Meadowhawks (Genus *Sympetrum*)
150 Black Meadowhawk
152 Band-winged Meadowhawk
153 Cherry-faced Meadowhawk
154 Ruby Meadowhawk
156 Saffron-winged Meadowhawk
158 White-faced Meadowhawk
160 Yellow-legged Meadowhawk
162 Variegated Meadowhawk

Elfin Skimmer (Genus *Nannothemis*)
164 Elfin Skimmer

Blue Dasher (Genus *Pachydiplax*)
166 Blue Dasher

Pondhawks (Genus *Erythemis*)
168 Eastern Pondhawk

Rainpool Gliders (Genus *Pantala*)
170 Spot-winged Glider
171 Wandering Glider

Whitefaces (Genus *Leucorrhinia*)
172 Dot-tailed Whiteface
174 Canada Whiteface
175 Hudsonian Whiteface
176 Crimson-ringed Whiteface
178 Red-waisted Whiteface
180 Frosted Whiteface

Small Pennants (Genus *Celithemis*)
182 Calico Pennant
183 Halloween Pennant

Saddlebag Gliders (Genus *Tramea*)
184 Black Saddlebags

Four-spotted Skimmer *Libellula quadrimaculata*

| MA | | SEPT | OCT | NOV |

Small, boggy lakes and ponds, marshes and some very slow streams. Prefers acidic waters.

Nature Notes:

The Four-spotted Skimmer is a circumpolar species whose range stretches across North America, Europe, down to northwestern Africa and over to Japan.

Juveniles range far from their home waters.

They prefer to perch on twigs or taller emergent vegetation but will alight in grasses or on the ground.

Description: Adults average 1.7 inches long.

Adults: All four wings have an amber patch along the leading edge ↑, a small, black nodal spot and a black stigma ↑. The hindwings also have black basal spots interwoven with yellow veins ↑. The abdomen is yellow-brown and somewhat transparent down to segment 6; segments 7 to 10 are black. Yellow abdominal side spots form a stripe down the length of the abdomen. Very mature individuals lose most of the amber color from their tattered wings and the abdomen becomes very drab and dark.

Juveniles: Young are often more brightly colored than mature adults.

Similar Species: Other species may have spots on their wings but none could be easily confused with a Four-spotted.

Tip-top perches on rushes, reeds and cattails are this skimmer's favorite place to launch aerial attacks on insect prey.

Hunting Technique: Four-spotted Skimmers are formidable predators and will even prey on other dragonflies, such as meadowhawks.

Mating & Egg Laying: Mating usually occurs in flight and lasts from a few seconds to more than a minute. The female oviposits single eggs but often with the male hover-guarding to protect her from other males and to safeguard the egg laying site from competing females. Male-male clashes for females are not uncommon.

Larvae: The eggs, when first deposited, are white. They soon turn brown and hatch in about five days depending upon the water temperature.

See the Four-spotted's four spots? In silhouette it is easy to pick out the black nodus and stigma on each wing. Also note the hindwing's large black and amber basal patch.

Slaty Skimmer *Libellula incesta* (male)

| MAY | JUNE | JULY | AUG | SEPT | OCT | NOV |

A variety of waters, but usually with mucky bottoms, sometimes sandy. Usually near forests. Occasionally boggy lakes.

Nature Notes:

The Slaty Skimmer perches horizontally on the tips of vertical twigs. Rarely perches on rocks, logs or the ground.

Description: Adults average 2 inches long.

Adults: Mature male is entirely dark blue ↑ except for his black face and dark brown eyes. In both sexes the abdomen is long and slender. The wings are also slender compared with most other larger skimmers. Female's thorax is brown in front, pale below while her abdomen has a dark brown to black stripe down the top with a yellowish-tan stripe along the sides. Female darkens with age to a uniform brown or grayish with pruinose cast, and her eyes become red-brown.

Juveniles: Both sexes resemble a young female.

Similar Species: Both the male Eastern Pondhawk and Blue Dasher have a pruinose blue abdomen and green eyes, but the former has a green thorax turning light blue while the latter has a striped green-and-black thorax. Neither is as dark as the Slaty Skimmer.

Juveniles of both sexes are colored as above, but mature female's body turns brown and may even develop some pruinosity.

Hunting Technique: Slaty Skimmers initiate feeding forays from twig perches along wooded edges.

Mating & Egg Laying: Males are most active in the morning and are very aggressive and territorial. Males perform competitive displays about one another, flying in horizontal loops around their opponents. Females are able to lay as many as 2000 eggs in one session.

Larvae: The aquatic nymphs prefer underwater habitats with a rich layer of rotting organic matter.

Twelve-spotted Skimmer *Libellula pulchella* (male)

| MAY | | OCT | NOV |

Ponds, lakes and bays with marshy borders. Slow streams and sometimes bogs. Prefers habitats with soft bottoms.

Nature Notes:

The Twelve-spotted seeks out a prominent perch, such as a stout branch or twig, for its home base and will return to it repeatedly, even when disturbed.

Description: Adults average 2 inches long.

Adults: Three large, black patches ↑ (base, nodus and wingtip) mark each of the four wings for a total of twelve. In addition, the male has white splotches between each black patch and a pair at the base of the hindwing (total of ten). On female the yellow side spots form a smooth stripe ↑ down each side of the abdomen, which tapers toward the tip.

Juveniles: Young look the same as females.

Similar Species: The female Common Whitetail has a nearly identical wing pattern to the female and juvenile Twelve-spotted, but the abdominal side spots of the Whitetail form a jagged, sawtooth-pattern, not a smooth stripe. The Prince Baskettail also has three black patches per wing, but it is a very long and slender dragonfly, unlike this chunky skimmer.

Yellow abdominal side stripes on both the male and female form a smooth, straight line. Compare to the jagged zigzag line of female and juvenile male Common Whitetails.

Flight Characteristics: The male's flight is accented by bursts of speed and sudden hovering stops followed by a hasty retreat in a completely different direction.

Mating & Egg Laying: Males fly irregular patrols, driving off any other dragonfly (Twelve-spotted or not) that enters its airspace. He sometimes hover-guards the female while she is ovipositing. If she is unguarded, interested males may harass her as she lays eggs. The female lays eggs by rapidly striking the tip of her abdomen on the water above submerged vegetation.

This male Twelve-spotted has found a perfect perch from which to launch his aerial feeding bouts and territorial defense attacks.

Common Whitetail *Plathemis (Libellula) lydia* (male)

MAY	JUNE	JULY	AUG	SEPT	OCT	NOV

Ponds, pools and quiet parts of lakes. Slow-stream pools and marshes. Prefers muddy bottoms with little clay.

Description: Adults average 1.7 inches long.

Nature Notes:

The aquatic nymphs prefer underwater habitats with a rich layer of rotting organic matter.

Juveniles venture away from water after emerging to hunt along woodland openings, roads and fields.

The Common Whitetail is primarily a ground percher.

Adults: Mature males have a striking white (pruinose) abdomen ↑. Wings of the male show a broad black band ↑ and a smaller black patch near the base. The female's wings each have three black patches. The abdomen is parallel-sided with a blunt tip. The female's abdomen is brown with whitish-yellow side spots that form a jagged, saw-toothed line ↑. Both sexes have a pair of yellow-white thoracic stripes.

Juveniles: Abdomens of all young look like the adult female's. Sexes have unique wing patterns.

Similar Species: The female Twelve-spotted Skimmer is nearly identical, but her abdomen gradually tapers to the tip, and the abdominal side spots form a straight line. The Prince

The yellow, abdominal side stripes of female (above) and young male whitetails form a jagged zigzag. Compare to the smooth side stripes of the female Twelve-spotted Skimmer.

Baskettail has wings patterned like the female but is much more slender and has green eyes.

Mating & Egg Laying:

Males ferociously defend territories over aquatic

Juvenile male showing typical male wing pattern and a non-pruinose body. It will turn white with age.

habitat that they deem suitable. Females who want to lay eggs within a certain territory are obliged to mate with the male who controls it. But a competing male may be able to swoop in and overtake the patrolling male's female and it is the last male to mate with a female who will be sire to her eggs. Aggressive males brandish their white abdomens to intimidate other males while the submissive males lower their tails in response. The female may lay up to 1,000 eggs in one day, and she may mate every day or two. She rhythmically strikes the water about once per second while the male hover-guards overhead. Each vigorous strike of her abdomen may send a drop of water up to a foot in the air.

Widow Skimmer *Libellula luctuosa* (male)

MAY			SEPT	OCT	NOV

Ponds, lakes and marshes. Not found in temporary or seasonally wet ponds.

Nature Notes:

The Widow Skimmer often perches on the tips of reeds.

During the night, Widow Skimmers hang beneath overarching leaves.

Description: Adults average 1.8 inches long.

Adult: The male's striking wing pattern is formed by black from base to nodus and a broad, white band ↑ that reaches from the black patch to the stigma of each wing. Females lack the white bands but do show black bases ↑. The abdomen of the male becomes gray and pruinose with maturity. The female's abdomen has a black top stripe, which is flanked by bright yellow side stripes that meet at the base of the abdomen.

Juveniles: Young of both sexes resemble females, but in the male the yellow abdominal stripes become increasingly drab and eventually obscured by pruinosity at maturity.

Similar Species: The Widow Skimmer's wing pattern is unmatched by any other species.

The immature male (above) and female do not show white wing patches. Both have a dark brown abdomen with an orangish stripe down each side. Adult females usually have smaller black wing patches than males and dusky wing tips.

Mating & Egg Laying: The males in a given population will achieve a pecking order that makes the dominant male the preferred mate. At lower population densities, a male may occupy a territory as large as 250 square yards. The female oviposits alone except when in a dense population, in which case the male hover-guards her to protect his "genetic investment."

Larvae: The eggs, when first deposited, are white. They soon turn brown and hatch in about five days, depending on the water temperature.

Chalk-fronted Corporal *Ladona (Libellula) julia* (male)

MAY	JUNE	JULY	AUG	SEPT	OCT	NOV

Boggy ponds, lake bays and slow forested streams. Prefer acidic conditions with abundant decaying bottom vegetation.

Nature Notes:

The Chalk-fronted Corporal is a very social creature, often congregating in great numbers on trails and boat docks. Given the opportunity, they will feast on the mosquitoes and deer flies that invariable accompany you in the field. I have had them perch on my shoulder while they chewed up an insect that was coming in for a human blood meal.

Description: Adults average 1.6 inches long.

Adults: Male has a dark body with obvious white or grayish pruinosity on front of thorax and first half of abdomen ↑. Markings on the front of the thorax form a pair of broad, white "corporal" stripes. Small, dark patches at the base of clear wings; hindwing patches are triangular and those on the forewing are smaller or entirely lacking. Female's body is dark brown and her pruinose markings are gray.

Juveniles: Young are orangey-brown with a black stripe down the top of the abdomen. A pair of narrow white stripes on the front of the thorax are where the broad "corporal" stripes will develop later.

Similar Species: Other skimmers of similar size with pruinose markings on the abdomen have bold patterning on their wings. Similarly

Though juvenile Chalk-fronted Corporals lack the "chalk" of pruinosity, the developing "corporal stripes" can be seen on their orange thorax.

patterned whitefaces and meadowhawks are much smaller and more slender.

Hunting Technique: Instead of flitting about in search of prey, the Chalk-fronted Corporal prefers to hunt while perched on the ground or a rock, waiting for prey to fly over and then pursuing. They frequent woodland openings, roads, yards, etc. before returning to water to breed.

Mating & Egg Laying: Female is able to lay eggs without a male guarding her. Males aggressively chase one another over open water. Maturing individuals do not return to the breeding waters until their white pruinose markings are nearly fully developed.

Larvae: Aquatic nymphs prefer habitats with a rich layer of rotting organic matter.

Nature Notes:

There is an ongoing discussion as to whether Chalk-fronted Corporals should be in the genus *Libellula* or placed in the *Ladona*. Depending upon the source, it could be listed as either.

Black Meadowhawk *Sympetrum danae* (male)

MAY	JUNE	JU			OCT	NOV

Marshy or boggy ponds and sometimes small lakes.

Nature Notes:

The Black Meadowhawk is the only member of the genus *Sympetrum* that has a circumpolar range; it is well known in Northern Europe and in Asia.

Named in 1776, this was the first meadowhawk to be scientifically described.

They have been seen migrating in large numbers off the coast of Ireland, but I've seen no literature suggesting that large migrations occur in North America.

Description: Adults average 1.2 inches long.

Adults: No red coloration at all; mature male is all black including his face ↑. Mature female is yellow and black with complex markings on the sides of her thorax ↑. Black markings on the female's abdomen surround at least the last eight segments at the joints. Sometimes there are pale amber patches at the bases of the hindwings and a pale amber region near the nodus of the forewings. Legs and stigma are black.

Similar Species: The female Elfin Skimmer is black and yellow like the female Black Meadowhawk, but it is much smaller and has larger amber patches at wing bases. The early-emerging Ebony Boghaunter is about the same size but has light-colored abdominal rings on segments 2 to 4 only.

Note the complex thoracic markings. They are the same on females and juvenile males.

Mating & Egg Laying: The Black Meadowhawk is not an early riser and mating doesn't seem to get started until at least midday. The female lays eggs in ponds, either in tandem or alone, following no set rhythm or pattern.

Band-winged Meadowhawk *Sympetrum semicinctum*

MAY	JUNE	JULY	AUG	SEPT	OCT	NOV

Small, spring-fed ponds and flooded marshes with slow current.

Nature Notes:

The Band-winged is not a very widespread species, and it is only common locally where its specific habitat is found.

The larvae do not compete well with other dragonflies and are susceptible to predation by fish.

Description: Adults average 1.3 inches long.

Adults: The inner halves of both wings are colored with yellow-brown bands ↑, which are visible in flight. Thorax is reddish brown with brown hairs. Black side triangles on abdomen are low, forming a jagged line. Top of the abdomen is red in mature individuals; females sometimes remain yellow. Legs all black.

Juveniles: Abdomen of young is brown with a black stripe down the side.

Similar Species: None. Wing bands are diagnostic amongst the meadowhawks.

Mating & Egg Laying: Egg laying takes place amongst emergent vegetation while female is in tandem with the male.

Cherry-faced Meadowhawk *Sympetrum internum*

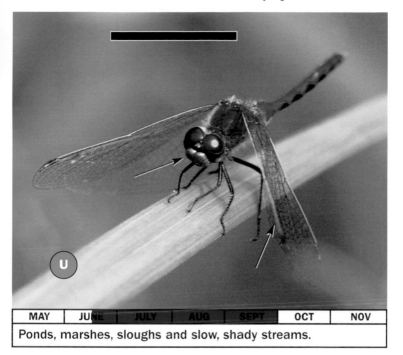

| MAY | JUNE | JULY | AUG | SEPT | OCT | NOV |

Ponds, marshes, sloughs and slow, shady streams.

Description: Adults average 1.3 inches long.

Adults: Red face is distinctive in adults ↑. Stigma are paler towards the wingtips. Amber patch at wing bases. Veins at leading edge of wing are orange ↑. High, black triangles on the sides of the bright red abdomen. Legs are black.

Juveniles: Abdomen of young is yellow-brown and its face is yellowish.

Similar Species: Identification of red *Sympetrums* is tricky at best and often impossible in the field. The Saffron-winged Meadowhawk has a uniformly light-colored stigma, black and red-striped legs, pale red abdomen and the leading edges of the wings are amber. The Yellow-legged Meadowhawk has yellow-striped legs and reduced black side-triangles on the abdomen.

Nature Notes:

Cherry-faced Meadowhawks can be seen laying eggs in mowed lawns far from water. Why? They choose grassy sites that they believe will be inundated with water. Sometimes they choose wrong!

Ruby Meadowhawk *Sympetrum rubicundulum* (male)

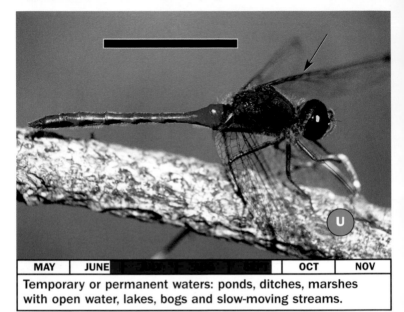

| MAY | JUNE | | | | OCT | NOV |

Temporary or permanent waters: ponds, ditches, marshes with open water, lakes, bogs and slow-moving streams.

Description: Adults average 1.4 inches long.

Adults: Note the yellowish-brown face ↑ and black wing veins ↑. Abdomen is red in mature male and yellowish in female; both have black triangles down the side. Stigma are paler towards the wingtips, and there is a small amber patch at the wing bases. Black legs. Male's claspers are red.

Nature Notes:

From the tips of their grassy perches, male Rubies defend tiny territories of about six feet in diameter.

Juveniles: Young's abdomen is yellow-brown.

Similar Species: Essentially inseparable in the field from Cherry-faced and juvenile White-faced Meadowhawks. The Saffron-winged Meadowhawk has uniformly light colored stigma, black and red-striped legs, a pale red abdomen and the leading edges of the wings are amber. Yellow-legged Meadowhawk has brownish legs and reduced black side-triangles on the abdomen.

Mating & Egg Laying: Female lays eggs by repeatedly dipping her abdomen into the

Remember, field identification of meadowhawks is extremely difficult (some can only be identified in the lab under a microscope), so if stumped, be content to simply call it a "red meadowhawk" or a *Sympetrum* species and leave it at that.

water, or by simply dropping the eggs from the air into the water or along a shoreline. The male usually accompanies the female during egg laying (sometimes joined in tandem) and seems to direct her efforts.

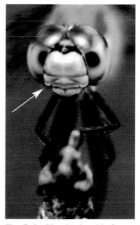

The Ruby Meadowhawk's face remains yellow-brown throughout its adult life.

Saffron-winged Meadowhawk *Sympetrum costiferum*

MAY	JUNE	JULY	AUG	SEPT	OCT	NOV

Reedy marshes bordering ponds with solid bottoms. Also occasionally found in boggy habitats.

Nature Notes:

Large congregations of Saffron-winged Meadowhawks have been observed sitting on power lines all facing the same direction.

The Saffron-winged is not as easily approached as other meadowhawks.

Description: Adults average 1.4 inches long.

Adults: The leading edge of each wing is gold (saffron) ↑ except in older adults (especially males), yet the veins remain reddish or orange. Stigma are solid in color, either red or yellow. Side of abdomen has low, black triangles ↑ that form a black stripe. Black spots on the tops of abdominal segments 8 and 9. The legs are striped lengthwise with yellow and black except in older adults, which are striped with red and black. Female is yellow and has a very light yellow to almost white face.

Similar Species: The Cherry-faced Meadowhawk has a bi-colored stigma, black, unstriped legs and high black triangles along the sides of the abdomen. Yellow-legged Meadowhawks have lighter legs and reduced black side-triangles on their abdomen.

Females and juvenile males both have a brownish-orange abdomen, a dull yellow face and brown thorax.

Mating & Egg Laying: May lay eggs in tandem or solo. Female dips her abdomen repeatedly and deliberately into shallow water to deposit eggs. The male guards the female from the advances of any male interloper.

Saffron-colored wing veins and stigma seem to glow in the right light.

Genus *Sympetrum* MEADOWHAWKS

White-faced Meadowhawk *Sympetrum obtrusum*

MAY	JU						NOV

Temporary to permanent ponds, marshes, bogs, lakes and slow streams. Adult is associated with forests.

Nature Notes:

Males will fly in tandem with a female Cherry-faced Meadowhawk or a female Ruby Meadowhawk but actual matings are rare, as the reproductive parts are not compatible (like a lock and a key). Look for this "extra-specific" coupling when you see a male White-faced Meadowhawk flying in tandem, but not in wheel formation, with a female.

Description: Adults average 1.3 inches long.

Adults: Mature White-faced Meadowhawks have pearly white faces ↑. Male's abdomen is bright red; female's abdomen is yellow-orange. Both show distinct black triangles along the sides of the abdomen. They do not have amber patches at their wing bases. Black legs.

Similar Species: Mature Cherry-faced Meadowhawks and Ruby Meadowhawks both look similar but do not have white faces. Juveniles of these three species are not readily distinguishable from one another.

Mating & Egg Laying: During mating, the male and female tend to fly in tandem when the air is warm, but the male merely hover-guards her in cooler weather. The female drops her eggs into shallow water or on mud amongst shoreline vegetation. Egg laying occurs later in the day in grassy habitats that

Juvenile White-faced Meadowhawks are impossible to distinguish from Ruby Meadowhawks. Juvenile Cherry-faced Meadowhawks show amber wing veins at their leading edge.

have the potential to be flooded. The eggs overwinter and hatch in the spring. They often overestimate the potential for flooding, as it is not unusual to observe them laying eggs in grassy lawns, far from water.

In the morass of confusion that is meadowhawk identification, the white face of the White-faced is a welcome field mark. It is the only meadowhawk species that has a pearly white face.

Yellow-legged Meadowhawk *Sympetrum vicinum*

MAY	JUNE	JULY	AUG	SEPT	OCT	NOV

Slow streams, permanent ponds, bogs and marshes.

Nature Notes:

Yellow-leggeds have the latest flight period of any dragonfly in the North Woods; they are often sighted into November if we've had no hard freezes. They can fly and feed in temperatures slightly below 50 degrees F.

Yellow-leggeds usually occupy higher perches than other meadowhawks, who often prefer to perch on the ground.

Often seen locally in very large numbers.

Description: Adults average 1.3 inches long.

Adults: Look for the light legs ↑ (brown to orangish) that separate this species from other meadowhawks who have black legs. The abdomen is red with no distinct black triangles ↑, though some black smudges may appear where abdominal triangles are normally found on other meadowhawks. Face is red. Wings are clear except at the very bases where they are tinted amber. Mature females are red like the male but have a prominent, trumpet-shaped ovipositor ↑ when viewed from the side.

Juveniles: Young are dusky, orangish-yellow and have no black triangles on their abdomen. Face is tan to yellow.

Similar Species: All other northern meadowhawks have dark legs and distinct black markings along the sides of their abdomen.

Note the female's prominent egg spout at the tip of her abdomen.

Mating & Egg Laying: Female dips her abdomen into shallow water, then onto muddy banks or grass stems, then back to water and so on. Because of this action, her abdomen is often covered in mud. Eggs overwinter, then hatch in the spring when the water is high.

Larvae: The majority of the aquatic nymphs emerge in August.

Yellow-legged Meadowhawks have brownish, yellowish or orangish legs—never black like most of their meadowhawk cousins. Also note the red face and red stigma.

Variegated Meadowhawk *Sympetrum corruptum* (male)

MAY	JUNE	JULY	AUG	SEPT	OCT	NOV

Almost any available aquatic habitat, except bogs or acid fens.

Nature Notes:

Don't set out to impress anyone by capturing a Variegated Meadowhawk, as it may make a fool of you. This is one of the most difficult dragonflies to net; it is very shy and wary (and seems to possess a level of telepathic ability).

Description: Adults average 1.5 inches long.

Adults: The male's striking abdomen is banded red and silver ↑ while the female's is coppery-rust, silver and white ↑. Two white thoracic side-stripes (yellow at their lower ends and reduced to just two yellow dots in mature male). Male's face is red; female's face is tan. Veins in leading edges of wings are light colored, orange in male, more yellow in female. All stigma are yellow on both ends and dark in the center. Legs are black with yellow lengthwise stripes.

Similar Species: Saffron-winged Meadowhawks also have light-colored wing veins, but the Saffron's abdomen is solid red. The Spot-winged Glider has a spot on the hindwing, whereas the smaller Variegated Meadowhawk has clear wings with light veins along the leading edges.

Variegated Meadowhawks make eastward migrations in the fall. This female was photographed in Duluth in the fall. She may have ended up on the East Coast or in the Florida Keys!

Life Cycle: Migrating Variegated Meadowhawks may be seen very early in the spring as they move north in large groups. They also migrate from the western parts of the country towards the East later in the summer.

Elfin Skimmer *Nannothemis bella* (male)

MAY	JU NE	JULY	AUG	SEPT	OCT	NOV

Floating bogs with low sedge growth, particularly calcareous (high pH) waters with marly (calcium-rich) bases.

Nature Notes:

This is North America's smallest dragonfly and the second smallest species in the world. (The smallest species is *Nannophyopsis clara*, which is found in China.)

They frequent areas with short vegetation such as Leatherleaf, Bog Rosemary, cotton-grasses and sedges.

When perched, the wings are thrust down and forward (see photos).

This is the only species in the genus *Nannothemis*. They are unique in their reduced wing venation.

Description: Adults average 0.8 inches long.

Adults: Our tiniest dragonfly ↑. Male is pruinose gray-blue with clear wings. Female is black-and-yellow striped, resembling a wasp ↑. Her wings have faint amber patches at the bases. The forewing "triangle" is not a triangle but is four-sided.

Juveniles: Young male is black, becoming pruinose in four to five days.

Similar Species: Tiny size easily distinguishes this dragonfly from all others.

Flight Characteristics: Elfins perch often and never fly very far when flushed.

Hunting Technique: They hunt in open, wet areas.

Mating & Egg Laying: When not in the act of mating, males patrol suitable egg-laying waters. Eggs are laid in warm, shallow waters with the pair in tandem or the male guarding nearby.

The striped yellow-and-black female resembles a small wasp with a narrow abdomen.

Blue Dasher *Pachydiplax longipennis* (male)

MAY				SEPT	OCT	NOV

Lakes, ponds and very slow streams. Rarely in bogs.

Nature Notes:

Both the male and female defend preferred feeding perches.

Adults will move short distances in small swarms to colonize new habitats.

The aquatic nymphs are very active, and they develop quickly.

Blue Dashers are migratory on the East Coast.

Description: Adults range from 1 to 1.7 inches long.

Adults: Mature male and female have a pale blue abdomen ↑ with a striking green and black striped thorax ↑. They both have a white face and amber patches on the wings. Also show two short black stripes at the base of the hindwings.

Juveniles: Younger female is dark brown with yellow markings on the thorax and abdomen. Her abdominal top spots are pairs of yellow dashes that do not reach segment 10.

Similar Species: The male Eastern Pondhawk also turns powdery blue in maturity, but its pruinosity also covers the unstriped thorax and his face is green.

Hunting Technique: Blue Dashers make short sallies from favorite perches to capture passing prey or to chase away intruders.

The pairs of yellow dashes on the top of the female's abdomen do not reach segment 10.

Mating & Egg Laying: Maturing males return to the water before the females. Females not actively seeking mates or laying eggs are likely found in nearby woods, feeding and avoiding aggressive males. Competing males attempt to intimidate each other by flashing their blue abdomens. When skirmishing, they attempt to fly below their opponents, quickly rising to push the other male upward and away from the water. Mating takes from twenty seconds to two minutes to complete. The male hover-guards the female while she lays eggs. When ovipositing, she flys extremely close to the water, striking the tip of her abdomen on the surface without changing the elevation of the rest of her body.

Blue Dashers have favorite perches from which they launch their hunting forays.

Eastern Pondhawk *Erythemis simplicicollis* (male)

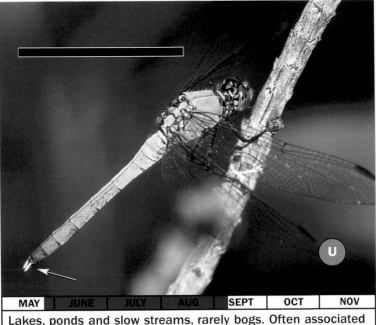

MAY	JUNE	JULY	AUG	SEPT	OCT	NOV

Lakes, ponds and slow streams, rarely bogs. Often associated with lily pads, duckweed and mats of floating algae.

Nature Notes:

Northern adults are believed to be somewhat migratory.

The Eastern Pondhawk spends nights hunkered down amongst grassy vegetation along shorelines, in meadows or roadside ditches.

During maturation the pruinosity starts at the tip of the abdomen and extends forward.

Description: Adults average 1.7 inches long.

Adults: Mature male has powder-blue pruinosity over entire thorax and abdomen. His face is green, eyes are blue-green and claspers white ↑. Female is bright green with black markings ↑. Her green thorax is unstriped. Ovipositor is spout-like. In both sexes the abdomen narrows at segment 4 or 5. Formidable spines on legs.

Juveniles: Young are similar to adult female.

Similar Species: The male Blue Dasher also attains a powder blue abdomen but retains his striped thorax throughout life. From a distance, the semimature male Eastern Pondhawk can resemble a Common Green Darner, but the darner is almost twice its size. Snaketails have separated eyes.

Flight Characteristics: Two males perform a dramatic flight in which they fly inches

Is this the same species as the male pictured on the other page? Yes, the female is quite different than the male. Her striped green and black abdomen is an eye-catcher.

above the water, one in front of the other. As if on cue, the front pondhawk drops down and back while the other scoots to the forward position. This repeats itself over and over.

Hunting Technique: Often described as our most ferocious dragonfly, the Eastern Pondhawk will eat anything its size or smaller. Dashing from a perch, it makes quick meals of damselflies, butterflies, moths or even other Eastern Pondhawks! Large leg spines assist in holding larger prey. They will follow behind large animals (including humans) to feed on swarming insects.

Mating & Egg Laying: Female dips her abdomen into water at intervals, dispensing as many as 2100 eggs in a day.

Fearsome hunters, the pondhawk will even capture and eat other pondhawks!

Spot-winged Glider *Pantala hymenaea* (male)

MAY	JUNE	JULY	AUG	SEPT	OCT	NOV

Temporary pools and ponds, sometimes slowly moving water.
Usually found near open, sunny waters.

Nature Notes:

The Spot-winged Glider is migratory in our range, arriving in summer from points south. The larvae can develop in as little as five weeks, and the new adults return south.

They range throughout the Americas, from Canada south to Argentina.

Description: Adults average 1.9 inches long.

Adults: Large, broad wings (especially hindwings), with small, dark, rounded patches near the base of the hindwing ↑ (sometimes faint). Tapering abdomen patterned with tan, brown and rust. Face is yellow to orange, red in mature male.

Juveniles: Young resemble adult female.

Similar Species: The Wandering Glider has no dark spot at base of the hindwing. Lighter-colored Variegated Meadowhawk looks similar in flight but is smaller with lighter wing veins.

Hunting Technique: Spot-winged Gliders feed all day long with less gliding and hovering than the Wandering Glider. They perch on higher twigs when resting.

Mating & Egg Laying: Males are very aggressive towards other males and even other species of dragonflies. When in tandem, the pair will drop suddenly, splashing water and dropping eggs, then move on to another spot.

Wandering Glider *Pantala flavescens* (male)

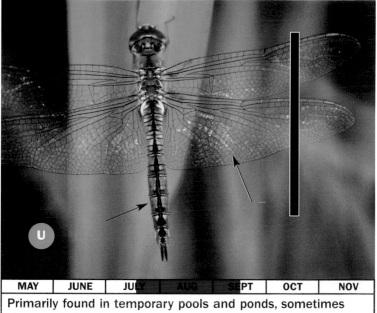

MAY	JUNE	JULY	AUG	SEPT	OCT	NOV

Primarily found in temporary pools and ponds, sometimes slow-moving water.

Description: Adults average 1.9 inches long.

Adults: Yellow abdomen ↑. Large and broad wings that lack spots ↑. Wingtips may become brown at maturity. Tapering, yellow abdomen has black top markings. Face is yellow becoming reddish in mature male.

Similar Species: The Spot-winged Glider has a dark spot near the base of the hindwing.

Flight Characteristics: May fly day and night for thousands of miles. Hover often.

Hunting Technique: Feed on swarms of insects over open fields.

Mating & Egg Laying: Males patrol territories of ten to fifty yards at a height of six feet.

Life Cycle: The Wandering Glider is migratory in our range, arriving in midsummer from points south. The larvae develop in about two months and the new adults return south.

Nature Notes:

The Wandering Glider is the only dragonfly known to occur on all the world's continents (except Antarctica). Though it can be found in Europe, it does not breed there.

This globe-trotting species is aptly used as the logo for the World Dragonfly Association.

It has been collected hundreds of miles from land on the decks of ocean-going vessels.

Considered our most highly evolved dragonfly species.

Dot-tailed Whiteface *Leucorrhinia intacta* (male)

| MAY | JUNE | JULY | AUG | SEPT | OCT | NOV |

Ponds, small lakes and quiet streams. Often found in conjunction with water-lilies. Sometimes found in boggy waters.

Description: Adults average 1.3 inches long.

Adults: The white face ↑, black body and conspicuous squarish yellow spot on segment 7 ↑ make this dragonfly distinct. Females may have light yellow markings preceding the spot on segment 7. Basal patches on hindwings have dark venation.

Juveniles: Young have yellow spots on top of abdomen segments 1 to 7; spot on segment 7 is squarish. Yellow spots on the sides of abdomen to segment 6.

Similar Species: Juvenile and female Hudsonian Whitefaces look very much like juvenile Dot-tails except that the Hudsonians have a distinctly triangular spot on segment 7 and light-colored veins in the basal patch on the hindwing.

Nature Notes:

One of the first dragonflies to emerge in the spring. They are often on the wing by mid May.

Juveniles are quite colorful compared to mature adults. But only the square spot on segment 7 will remain at maturity.

Only a small percentage of females show amber-tinted wings as in this one.

Mating & Egg Laying: The female lays eggs near aquatic plants that come in contact with the water's surface. The male hover-guards the female from a position above and a little behind her. Males are often seen perched on floating vegetation in the middle of a pond far from shore. They defend territories that are two to four meters wide.

Dot-tailed Whitefaces frequently perch on the ground.

Genus *Leucorrhinia* WHITEFACES

Canada Whiteface *Leucorrhinia patricia* (male)

MAY	JU		AUG	SEPT	OCT	NOV

Fens, bog ponds with floating edges and lakes with shallows.
Always acidic waters.

Nature Notes:

The Canada is a true boreal forest species.

It is very wary, watching for approaching danger from its perch on the tip of a low branch.

Description: Adults average 1.1 inches long.

Adults: Our smallest *Leucorrhinia* species. Red top of thorax ↑ and red abdominal top spots on segments 1 to 3; the rest are reduced to thin lines or are missing altogether. Abdomen mostly dark ↑. White face and black chin. Mature male is red and female is similarly patterned in yellow.

Juvenile: Young resemble adult female.

Similar Species: The larger Hudsonian has top spots past segment 3. The female Canada is the only whiteface with no top spot on segment 7.

Life Cycle: Entire flight period at any one site may be as short as two weeks.

Hudsonian Whiteface *Leucorrhinia hudsonica* (male)

MA			SEPT	OCT	NOV

Bogs and fens. Cold marshy waters. Adults prefer habitats with low-growing emergent vegetation.

Description: Adults average 1.2 inches long.

Adults: Red abdominal top spots on segments 1 to 8. Dark basal patch of hindwings has light venation ↑ except in very mature male. White face. Female is patterned as male except that top spots are pale yellow.

Nature Notes:

The male defends a territory of about one square meter.

Similar Species: Juvenile Dot-taileds have a squarish top spot on segment 7 instead of the triangular spot ↑ on female/juvenile Hudsonians.

Mating & Egg Laying: Using his claspers, male picks up the female by her neck. Copulation occurs in flight. The released female oviposits by quickly tapping her abdomen on the surface of the water while the male hovers protectively nearby, thwarting competing suitors.

Look for the triangular top spot on segment 7 of juvenile Hudsonians.

Crimson-ringed Whiteface *Leucorrhinia glacialis* (male)

MAY	JUNE	JULY	AUG	SEPT	OCT	NOV

Boggy lakes and permanent marshes.

Nature Notes:

In my opinion, one of the most beautiful of all the dragonflies.

As in most dragonflies, their colors are not true pigments, but are the result of biological action. The vibrancy fades away shortly after death.

Description: Adults average 1.4 inches long.

Adults: Male shows brilliant red on top of his thorax. The abdomen is entirely black ↑. Female has pale, thin yellow abdominal top spots that reach no farther than a small spot on segment 7. White face. Cross-vein in the forewing's radial planate forms a double row of cells ↑.

Juvenile: Young male has yellow thoracic markings and an all black abdomen. Young female resembles adult female except that her yellow is more vivid.

Similar Species: Male Red-waisted Whiteface's abdomen turns white on the front half with age (pruinosity).

Hunting Technique: Hunts from a low perch or the ground, in sunlight or shade.

Mating & Egg Laying: Males defend territories from a low perch at the water's edge or from floating vegetation.

Young males show bright yellow on abdominal segments 1 to 4. This area will turn bright red as they mature. Young females have some yellow on segments 1 to 7.

Approaching a Crimson-ringed from the side or front you can easily see the characteristic white face that the group is named for. But this trait may not be visible from behind.

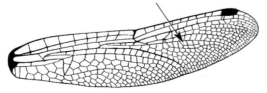

A cross-vein in the forewing's radial planate forms a double row of cells (highlighted). This trait separates the Crimson-ringed from the Red-waisted, which has a single row of cells here.

Red-waisted Whiteface *Leucorrhinia proxima* (male)

MA			UG	SEPT	OCT	NOV

Boggy lakes and ponds. Permanent marshes.

Nature Notes:

The Red-waisted Whiteface may disappear when the sun dips behind a cloud; when full sunlight returns, so will the Red-waisted. This is true for many dragonfly species, which need solar heating for optimal flight efficiency.

Description: Adults average 1.4 inches long.

Adults: Long, skinny abdomen is whitish at the base (pruinose) ↑ in fully mature individuals. Male has red patch on the back at the base of the forewings ↑. White face. Yellow-form female has thin, pale muddy-yellow top spots down to segment 7. Red-form female has reddish-orange spots. On wings there are three rows of cells in the region just beyond the forewing triangle ↑.

Juveniles: Young show a yellow thorax. Male has a black abdomen, which is yellow at its base. Young female has thin yellow top spots to segment 7.

Similar Species: The male Frosted Whiteface has no red on the back between the wings and has less pruinosity on its stubbier abdomen. Both sexes also differ from the Frosted by having three rows of cells, as

All Red-waisted Whitefaces start out with a yellow thorax, which in time turns brown and, at maturity, red. Females can be red or yellow.

opposed to the Frosted that has two rows in the region just beyond the forewing triangle. Crimson-ringed Whiteface has a double row of cells in the wing's radial planate, as opposed to the Red-waisted's single row of cells.

Hunting Technique: The Red-waisted hunts from a low perch or the ground in woodland openings.

Mating & Egg Laying: Male territories are one to two square yards and are defended by males perched in shrubs at water's edge.

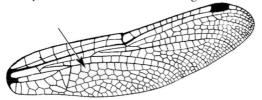

The triple row of cells just beyond the forewing triangle (highlighted) separates this species from the Frosted Whiteface which only has two rows of cells.

Frosted Whiteface *Leucorrhinia frigida* (male)

MAY	JUNE	JULY	AUG	SEPT	OCT	NOV

Boggy ponds, especially those with mats of floating sphagnum moss.

Nature Notes:

Frosted Whiteface's range is restricted to the North Woods of New England and the Great Lakes.

Description: Adults average 1.2 inches long.

Adults: Whitish, pruinose patch ↑ at the base of the stocky black abdomen with no red markings at all. Thorax is yellow with black spots (yellow turns to brown in maturity). White face. Female has pale, thin top spots on abdomen that get smaller as they go down the abdomen. Only two rows of cells in the region beyond the forewing triangle ↑.

Juveniles: Young male has rich yellow top spots, which get smaller as they go down the abdomen. Female juvenile's markings are muddier yellow.

Similar Species: The Frosted Whiteface never has red markings. Compare to the Red-waisted Whiteface, as the females and juveniles can be difficult to differentiate. The larger Chalk-fronted Corporal also has a white area

The mating wheel of a non-pruinose (yellow thorax) female (left) and a typical pruinose male.

at the base of its abdomen, but look for the pruinose "corporal stripes " on the top of the thorax. Red-waisteds have three rows of cells in the area just beyond the forewing triangle.

Hunting Technique: The Frosted hunts from a perch on low plants along the water's edge. May also pursue prey through low vegetation, zipping through the maze of stems.

Mating & Egg Laying: Males defend territories of about one to two yards from their perch on low plants or lily pads.

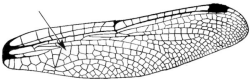

The double row of cells just beyond the forewing triangle (highlighted) separates this species from the Red-waisted.

Calico Pennant *Celithemis elisa* (male)

FC

| MAY | JUNE | JULY | AUG | SEPT | OCT | NOV |

Marshy or boggy ponds, slow streams and lakes with shallow soft-bottomed edges and emergent vegetation such as rushes.

Nature Notes:

The stunning little Calico Pennant is one of my favorites. Look for the males perched atop rushes in the shallows of lakes and ponds.

After 1999's legendary Fourth of July windstorm that leveled much of the Boundary Waters, Calico Pennants were all over the place, whereas they had not been found here before. In the years following, I have found them several other times in northeastern Minnesota. Will they stay or disappear after a few years because of an unknown variable?

Description: Adults average 1.2 inches long.

Adults: The combination of tiny size, large heart-shaped, red abdominal top spots ↑ on segments 4 to 7 and wing spots and patches make the Calico Pennant easy to identify. Females and juveniles have yellow abdomen spots. Stigma and face are red in males and yellow in females. Male's claspers are red.

Similar Species: Halloween has tinted wings.

Mating & Egg Laying: Male Calico Pennants patrol at a height of about two feet above the water. They are not very territorial. Female lays eggs in tandem with male, tapping her abdomen regularly on the water.

Larvae: The larvae of the genus *Celithemis* do not compete well with other dragonfly larvae. Therefore, look for them in newly formed ponds and borrow pits where other species have not yet established populations.

Halloween Pennant *Celithemis eponina* (male)

FC

MAY	JUNE	JULY	AUG	SEPT	OCT	NOV

Ponds, lakes and slow streams. Also newly formed ponds and ditches.

Description: Adults average 1.5 inches long.

Adults: Unmistakable. Orangish wings with numerous brown-black bands ↑ (hence the moniker, "Halloween"). Mature males and some females have an orange-red face and body markings. Most females have yellow marks.

Similar Species: No other band-winged species has tinted wings.

Flight Characteristics: The Halloween Pennant's flight is butterfly-like, with brightly-colored wings and bouncy flight.

Hunting Technique: Spends considerable time away from water, foraging above grassy slopes and openings.

Mating & Egg Laying: Males perch, pennant-like, on the tips of rushes. The mated pair flies straight up to a height of fifty feet. Lays eggs even on very windy days; the pair touches whitecaps to drop the eggs.

Nature Notes:

The Halloween Pennant seems to enjoy stiff winds and may be flying when other species seek shelter.

When perched, they hold their wings up at an angle with the forewings held higher than the hindwings.

Active on cooler days and even in drizzle or light rain, flinging water droplets from their wings when moving from perch to perch.

Halloweens are found all the way south to the Everglades of Florida.

Black Saddlebags *Tramea lacerata* (male)

MAY	JUNE	JULY	AUG	SEPT	OCT	NOV

Ponds, lakes and marshes, sometimes in temporary pools.
Prefers waters with rooted, submerged vegetation.

Nature Notes:

I have seen, though not captured, individual Black Saddlebags in Minnesota far north of its known range. The Red Saddlebags and Carolina Saddlebags have also been recorded in the North Woods.

During egg laying, the male releases the female so she can drop down to the water to release some eggs, whereupon she returns to the clutches of the male's claspers. This is done repeatedly.

Description: Adults average 2.1 inches long.

Adults: Large, irregular black patches on inner hindwings resemble saddlebags ↑. Abdomen is black with a pair of yellow abdominal top spots on segment 7. Abdominal appendages in both sexes are long and pointed.

Similar Species: The female Widow Skimmer also has black basal wing patches, but she has yellow abdominal side stripes.

Flight Characteristics: The flight of the Black Saddlebags is bouncy and punctuated by bursts of speed followed by leisurely gliding.

Hunting Technique: Often seen hawking insects over meadows and exposed hilltops.

Life Cycle: Spring individuals are likely adults that have migrated in from points south. Their progeny will emerge later in summer and migrate back south before the killing frosts of fall.

Common Damselflies

Damselflies (Suborder Zygoptera)

Closely related to dragonflies are the delicate damselflies. Damsels differ in wing shape (all four wings the same size and shape), resting posture (wings held up over their back—except in the *Lestes* spreadwings), separate eyes, a functional ovipositor and weak, fluttery flight. Nearly 40 species live in the North Woods. Below are a few of our most distinctive damsels.

Familiar Bluet
Enallagma civile

Familiar Bluet
Enallagma civile
(young)

Eastern Red Damsel
Amphiagrion saucium
(male)

Common Spreadwing
Lestes disjunctus

Eastern Forktail
Ischnura verticalis

Ebony Jewelwing
Calopteryx maculata
(male)

Ebony Jewelwing
Calopteryx maculata
(female)

River Jewelwing
Calopteryx aequabilis
(male)

River Jewelwing
Calopteryx aequabilis
(female)

Glossary

Abdomen: The elongated, ten-segmented rearward body part.

Abdominal segments: The ten separate parts that make up a dragonfly's abdomen.

Anisoptera: The suborder of Odonata containing the dragonflies.

Auricle: Outward-pointing knob on the second abdominal segment of some male dragonflies.

Cerci: Upper portion of the male's claspers.

Claspers: Grasping appendages at tip of males' abdomen, used to secure female during mating.

Epiproct: Lower portion of the male's claspers.

Exuviae: Shed skin left behind during the transformation from larva to adult.

Frons: Upper half of the dragonfly's face.

Hamules: Secondary male genitalia located underneath and within abdominal segment two.

Hawking: Hunting technique whereby a dragonfly flys off a prominent perch to catch an insect and promptly returns to that, or another perch.

In Copula: A mated pair of dragonflies engaged in copulation.

Juvenile: Life stage that occurs after the teneral stage; the body parts have hardened, but full coloration and sexual maturity have not yet been achieved.

Labium: The lower part of the mouth, sometimes called the "chin."

Labrum: The upper part of the mouth, sometimes considered the lower part of the face.

Larva: The aquatic first stage in the life of a dragonfly. Plural: larvae.

Nodus: Shallow notch located at about the midpoint of the wing's leading edge.

Nymph: The aquatic larva of a dragonfly.

Obelisking or Obelisk Position: When the tip of the abdomen is pointed directly at the sun to avoid overheating by reducing surface area exposed to solar radiation.

Occiput: The extreme upper part of the head behind the eyes.

Odonata: The Order containing both dragonflies and damselflies—the odonates.

Odonatist or Odonatologist: A person that studies dragonflies and damselflies.

Odonatology: The study of dragonflies and damselflies.

Ovipositor: The structure used by many female dragonflies to place eggs in a suitable environment.

Pruinosity: A white, waxy coating that develops on the bodies and wings of some mature dragonflies.

Shoulder: The region of the thorax below the forewing attachment point.

Stigma: The opaque patch, or cell, located at the front and towards the tip of each wing.

Suture: The connection line between two plates on the face or thorax.

Tandem: Position in which the male has the female grasped in his claspers. See also "Wheel."

Teneral: Life stage of the dragonfly just after it has emerged from the larval form, but before its wings and exoskeleton have hardened.

Thorax: The middle portion of the body to which the legs and wings are attached.

Wheel: The position of mating dragonflies when in tandem and the tip of the female's abdomen is locked into the male's hamules.

Zygoptera: The suborder of Odonata containing the damselflies.

Appendix A
Checklist of North Woods Dragonflies

Darners (Family Aeshnidae)

❏ Canada Darner	*Aeshna canadensis*	C
❏ Mottled Darner	*Aeshna clepsydra*	U
❏ Lance-tipped Darner	*Aeshna constricta*	FC
❏ Lake Darner	*Aeshna eremita*	FC
❏ Variable Darner	*Aeshna interrupta*	C
❏ Sedge Darner	*Aeshna juncea*	R
❏ Zigzag Darner	*Aeshna sitchensis*	R
❏ Subarctic Darner	*Aeshna subarctica*	R
❏ Black-tipped Darner	*Aeshna tuberculifera*	U
❏ Shadow Darner	*Aeshna umbrosa*	C
❏ Green-striped Darner	*Aeshna verticalis*	U
❏ Common Green Darner	*Anax junius*	C
❏ Springtime Darner	*Basiaeschna janata*	C
❏ Ocellated Darner	*Boyeria grafiana*	U
❏ Fawn Darner	*Boyeria vinosa*	C
❏ Swamp Darner	*Epiaeschna heros*	R
❏ Harlequin Darner	*Gomphaeschna furcillata*	R
❏ Cyrano Darner	*Nasiaeschna pentacantha*	U

Clubtails (Family Gomphidae)

❏ Horned Clubtail	*Arigomphus cornutus*	FC
❏ Lilypad Clubtail	*Arigomphus furcifer*	U
❏ Black-shouldered Spinyleg	*Dromogomphus spinosus*	C
❏ Mustached Clubtail	*Gomphus adelphus*	FC
❏ Lancet Clubtail	*Gomphus exilis*	FC
❏ Midland Clubtail	*Gomphus fraternus*	U
❏ Pronghorn Clubtail	*Gomphus graslinellus*	R
❏ Splendid Clubtail	*Gomphus lineatifrons*	U
❏ Ashy Clubtail	*Gomphus lividus*	FC
❏ Rapids Clubtail	*Gomphus quadricolor*	FC
❏ Dusky Clubtail	*Gomphus spicatus*	C
❏ Cobra Clubtail	*Gomphus vastus*	U
❏ Skillet Clubtail	*Gomphus ventricosus*	U
❏ Green-faced Clubtail	*Gomphus viridifrons*	U
❏ Dragonhunter	*Hagenius brevistylus*	C
❏ Extra-striped Snaketail	*Ophiogomphus anomalus*	R
❏ Riffle Snaketail	*Ophiogomphus carolus*	U
❏ Boreal Snaketail	*Ophiogomphus colubrinus*	FC
❏ Pygmy Snaketail	*Ophiogomphus howei*	U

❏ Sand Snaketail	*Ophiogomphus smithi*	VR
❏ Wisconsin Snaketail	*Ophiogomphus susbehcha*	R
❏ Rusty Snaketail	*Ophiogomphus rupinsulensis*	FC
❏ Common Sanddragon	*Progomphus obscurus*	U
❏ Least Clubtail	*Stylogomphus albistylus*	U
❏ Riverine Clubtail	*Stylurus amnicola*	U
❏ Elusive Clubtail	*Stylurus notatus*	R
❏ Zebra Clubtail	*Stylurus scudderi*	U
❏ Arrow Clubtail	*Stylurus spiniceps*	U

Spiketails (Family Cordulegasteridae)

❏ Brown Spiketail	*Cordulegaster bilineata*	VR
❏ Delta-spotted Spiketail	*Cordulegaster diastatops*	R
❏ Twin-spotted Spiketail	*Cordulegaster maculata*	C
❏ Arrowhead Spiketail	*Cordulegaster obliqua*	U

Cruisers (Family Macromiidae)

| ❏ Stream Cruiser | *Didymops transversa* | FC |
| ❏ Illinois River Cruiser | *Macromia illinoiensis* | FC |

Emeralds (Family Corduliidae)

❏ American Emerald	*Cordulia shurtleffii*	C
❏ Racket-tailed Emerald	*Dorocordulia libera*	FC
❏ Prince Baskettail	*Epicordulia (Epitheca) princeps*	C
❏ Stygian Shadowdragon	*Neurocordulia yamaskanensis*	U
❏ Ringed Emerald	*Somatochlora albicincta*	VR
❏ Lake Emerald	*Somatochlora cingulata*	R
❏ Ski-tailed Emerald	*Somatochlora elongata*	U
❏ Plains Emerald	*Somatochlora ensigera*	R
❏ Forcipate Emerald	*Somatochlora forcipata*	U
❏ Delicate Emerald	*Somatochlora franklini*	R
❏ Hine's Emerald	*Somatochlora hineana*	VR
❏ Hudsonian Emerald	*Somatochlora hudsonica*	VR
❏ Incurvate Emerald	*Somatochlora incurvata*	R
❏ Kennedy's Emerald	*Somatochlora kennedyi*	U
❏ Ocellated Emerald	*Somatochlora minor*	FC
❏ Clamp-tipped Emerald	*Somatochlora tenebrosa*	R
❏ Brush-tipped Emerald	*Somatochlora walshii*	FC
❏ Williamson's Emerald	*Somatochlora williamsoni*	FC
❏ Beaverpond Baskettail	*Tetragoneuria (Epitheca) canis*	C
❏ Common Baskettail	*Tetragoneuria (Epitheca) cynosura*	C
❏ Spiny Baskettail	*Tetragoneuria (Epitheca) spinigera*	C
❏ Ebony Boghaunter	*Williamsonia fletcheri*	U

Skimmers (Family Libellulidae)

❏ Calico Pennant	*Celithemis elisa*	FC
❏ Halloween Pennant	*Celithemis eponina*	FC
❏ Eastern Pondhawk	*Erythemis simplicicollis*	U
❏ Chalk-fronted Corporal	*Ladona (Libellula) julia*	C
❏ Frosted Whiteface	*Leucorrhinia frigida*	FC
❏ Crimson-ringed Whiteface	*Leucorrhinia glacialis*	FC
❏ Hudsonian Whiteface	*Leucorrhinia hudsonica*	FC
❏ Dot-tailed Whiteface	*Leucorrhinia intacta*	C
❏ Canada Whiteface	*Leucorrhinia patricia*	U
❏ Red-waisted Whiteface	*Leucorrhinia proxima*	FC
❏ Slaty Skimmer	*Libellula incesta*	U
❏ Widow Skimmer	*Libellula luctuosa*	FC
❏ Twelve-spotted Skimmer	*Libellula pulchella*	C
❏ Four-spotted Skimmer	*Libellula quadrimaculata*	C
❏ Elfin Skimmer	*Nannothemis bella*	U
❏ Blue Dasher	*Pachydiplax longipennis*	FC
❏ Wandering Glider	*Pantala flavescens*	U
❏ Spot-winged Glider	*Pantala hymenaea*	U
❏ Common Whitetail	*Plathemis (Libellula) lydia*	C
❏ Variegated Meadowhawk	*Sympetrum corruptum*	U
❏ Saffron-winged Meadowhawk	*Sympetrum costiferum*	FC
❏ Black Meadowhawk	*Sympetrum danae*	U
❏ Cherry-faced Meadowhawk	*Sympetrum internum*	U
❏ White-faced Meadowhawk	*Sympetrum obtrusum*	C
❏ Ruby Meadowhawk	*Sympetrum rubicundulum*	U
❏ Band-winged Meadowhawk	*Sympetrum semicinctum*	U
❏ Yellow-legged Meadowhawk	*Sympetrum vicinum*	C
❏ Carolina Saddlebags	*Tramea carolina*	R
❏ Black Saddlebags	*Tramea lacerata*	R
❏ Red Saddlebags	*Tramea onusta*	R

C	– Common	Encountered often and in many habitats.
FC	– Fairly Common	Fairly easy to find on a given day.
U	– Unusual	Never numerous. Must be in right habitat.
R	– Rare	Right time and right habitat may equal success.
VR	– Very Rare	Lucky to see one every few years.

Appendix B
World Synonyms

In North America we refer to an insect in the suborder Anisoptera as a "dragonfly"—certainly a strange image when you stop and think about it. But we certainly do not corner the market on bizarre names for these amazing critters. Strangely, many cultures around the globe have attributed evil to these innocent insects. Even the Swedes are guilty. One of their names for the dragonfly is *skams besman*, or "devil's-steel-yard." The reference is to an old weighing tool; they believed that when a dragonfly flew around your head, your soul was being weighed by the devil. Below is a list of colorful folk names from around the world.

North America
Mosquito-hawk
Snake-doctor
Darning-needle

England
Devil's darning-needle
Horse Stinger
Cow Killer
Ear Cutter
Balance Fly
Bee-butcher
Horse-adder
Adder's-needle
Lady Fly
Heather-flee
Jacky Breezer
Spinneroo
Spinning-Jenny
Bullstang

Wales
Gwas-y-neidr—Adder's-servant

Scotland
Damhan nathran — Ox-viper

Ireland
Spear adoir — Mower
Cleardhar coach — Blind Wasp
Spiogan mor — Big-spike

Germany
Teufelsnadel — Devil's-needle
Tuefelspferd — Devil's-horse
Wasserhexe — Water-witch
Hollenross — Goddess's-horse
Schlangentöter — Snake Killer
Augenstecher — Eye Sticker

Spain
Caballito del Diablo —
Devil's-horse

France
Demoiselle — Damsel
L'aiguille du diable —
Devil's-needle

Denmark
Guldsmed — Goldsmith
Fandens Ridehest —
Devil's riding-horse

Norway
Öyenstikker — Eye Sticker

Sweden
Trollslända — Hobgoblin Fly
Blindsticka — Blind Stinger
Skams Besman —
Devil's-steelyard

Appendix C
Phenology Flight Chart

Pg.	Species	April	May	June
46	Common Green Darner			
114	Beaverpond Baskettail			
172	Dot-tailed Whiteface			
112	Spiny Baskettail			
55	Springtime Darner			
93	Twin-spotted Spiketail			
89	Rusty Snaketail			
138	Four-spotted Skimmer			
110	Common Baskettail			
62	Dusky Clubtail			
100	Stream Cruiser			
106	American Emerald			
148	Chalk-fronted Corporal			
168	Eastern Pondhawk			
144	Common Whitetail			
142	Twelve-spotted Skimmer			
80	Horned Clubtail			
70	Skillet Clubtail			
84	Boreal Snaketail			
78	Black-shouldered Spinyleg			
183	Halloween Pennant			
115	Prince Baskettail			
116	Brush-tipped Emerald			
164	Elfin Skimmer			
58	Dragonhunter			
40	Variable Darner			
158	White-faced Meadowhawk			
26	Canada Darner			
50	Fawn Darner			
150	Black Meadowhawk			
160	Yellow-legged Meadowhawk			

July	August	September	October	November

Appendix D & E
Dragonfly Groups & Websites

International Odonata Research Institute
Comprehensive source for Odonata websites, collecting resources and dragonfly books. Contact information for most of the world's odonatists.

IORI c/o Florida Division of Plant Industry
1911 SW 34th Street, Gainesville FL 32608
http://www.afn.org/~iori/
(or at google.com type "Odonata Research Institute")

Michigan Odonata Survey
MOS c/o Museum of Zoology, Insect Division, University of Michigan
Ann Arbor, MI 48109-1079
The MOS publishes the newsletter *Williamsonia*.
http://insects.ummz.lsa.umich.edu/MICHODO/MOS.html
(or at google.com type "Michigan Odonata Survey")

World Dragonfly Association
WDA publishes the international journal *Pantala* and a newsletter, *Agrion*.
http://powell.colgate.edu/wda/dragonfly.htm
(or at google.com type "World Dragonfly Association")

Dragonfly Society of the Americas
DSA publishes the journal *American Odonatology* and a newsletter, *Argia*.
http://www.afn.org/~iori/dsaintro.html
(or at google.com type "Dragonfly Society of the Americas")

Photo Credits

Kurt Mead (mndfly@cpinternet.com): 2, 4mb, 12, 14, 15, 16, 17, 30, 31, 34, 35, 41t, 49b, 50, 51, 58, 59tb, 61, 63tb, 64, 65tb, 79mb, 80, 85tb, 88, 93, 95tb, 100, 101b, 102, 103b, 106, 108, 110, 117tb, 122, 127t, 133, 139tb, 152, 175t, 177tb, 178, 179, 186(3), 187(2,5).

Sparky Stensaas (sparkystensaas@hotmail.com): 6, 7, 9, 10, 13, 26, 27, 32, 33, 44, 45, 46, 47, 142, 143tb, 144, 145tb, 147, 148, 149, 158, 159tb, 160, 161tb, 162, 163, 166, 169tb, 172tb, 173tb, 180, 183, 186(1,2,4), 187(1,3,4).

Robbye Johnson (robbyejj@aol.com): 3, 4t, 5, 36, 37, 40, 41b, 42, 43, 55, 62, 70, 72, 77, 78tb, 79t, 81, 94, 101t, 103t, 107, 111, 116, 132, 138, 146, 167t, 171, 175b, 176, 181tb, 182.

Blair Nikula (odenews@odenews.net): 28, 38, 48, 49t, 52, 53, 66, 67, 71, 76, 82, 83, 87, 96, 109, 115, 118, 119, 120, 121, 126, 127b, 129, 130, 131, 134, 140, 141, 150, 154, 164, 165, 168, 170.

Sid Dunkle (sdunkle@ccccd.edu): 39, 54, 60, 69, 73, 74, 75, 84, 86, 90, 98, 123, 124, 125, 128, 174, 184.

John Webber (218. 652. 2535): 68, 89, 112, 113t, 114, 151, 153, 155tb, 156, 157tb, 167b.

Larry West (517. 676. 1890): 8

t=top, m=middle, b=bottom

Appendix F
Titles of Interest

Carpenter, V. 1991. *Dragonflies and Damselflies of Cape Cod*. Cape Cod Museum of Natural History. Natural History Series #4.

Corbet, P. S. 1999. *Dragonflies, Behavior and Ecology of Odonata*. Ithaca, NY: Cornell University Press.

Curry, J. R. 2001. *Dragonflies of Indiana*. Indiana Academy of Science.

Dunkle, S. 2000. *Dragonflies through Binoculars*. New York, NY: Oxford University Press.

Glotzhober, R. C., and D. McShaffrey. 2002. *The Dragonflies and Damselflies of Ohio*. Columbus, OH: Ohio Biological Survey.

Holder, M. 1996. *The Dragonflies and Damselflies of Algonquin Provincial Park*. Algonquin Park Tech. Bulletin #11.

Legler, K., D. Legler and D. Westover. 1996, 1998. *Color Guide to Common Dragonflies of Wisconsin*. (Self-published by Karl Legler: 429 Franklin Street, Sauk City, WI 53583).

Needham, J. G., M. J. Westfall and M. L. May. 2000. *Dragonflies of North America*. Gainesville, FL: Scientific Publishers, Inc.

Nikula, B., and J. Sones. 2002. *Stokes Beginner's Guide to Dragonflies*. Boston, MA: Little, Brown and Company.

Rosche, L. 2002. *Dragonflies and Damselflies of Northeast Ohio*. Cleveland, OH: Cleveland Museum of Natural History.

Shaw, J. 1987. *John Shaw's Closeups in Nature*. New York, NY: Amphoto.

Silsby, J. 2001. *Dragonflies of the World*. Washington D.C.: Smithsonian Institution Press.

Smith, W., T. Vogt and K. Gaines. 1993. *Checklist of Wisconsin Dragonflies*. Wisconsin Entomological Society. (Includes status, breeding habitat, range, and flight period.)

Walker, E. M., and P. S. Corbet. 1975. *The Odonata of Canada and Alaska, Volumes 1, 2 & 3*. Toronto, ON: Univ. Toronto Press. (This three volume set is available from: Toronto Entomologists' Assn. c/o Allan Hanks, 34 Seaton Drive, Aurora, ON Canada L4G 2K1)

Walton, R.K., and R.A. Forster. 1997. *Common Dragonflies of the Northeast*. (Video). (Available from: NHS, 7 Concord Greene #8, Concord, MA 01742)

West, L., and J. Ridl 1994. *How to Photograph Insects and Spiders*. Mechanicsburg, PA: Stackpole Books.

Appendix G
Binoculars for "Dragonflying"

Quality close-focusing optics have opened the door to the hobby of dragonfly watching or "dragonflying." Close-focusing is a must; full-size is preferable; power is a matter of choice. Listed here is a sampling of the best binoculars for watching our "winged dragons."

Weight is listed because some folks prefer lighter optics. The compacts are lighter, but they gather less light at dawn and dusk. They are also harder to hold steady than their full-size cousins. Compact binoculars are nice for easy packing on longer hikes.

Good dragonflying binoculars should focus under ten feet and preferably under six feet. This gives you the magnification to fill your field-of-view with the dragonfly.

The last column represents relative brightness. The higher the number the brighter your view will be. This is important for picking out details at dawn and dusk. Though brightness is not as big a deal as it is with birding binoculars, some dragonflies do fly at dusk when a brighter view would be a bonus.

What is the difference between 10-power and 8-power? With increased power one loses brightness. As stated above, this may not be a big problem with dragonflying. Also with higher power binoculars, any body movement is magnified.

Brand	size	weight (in oz.)	closest focus	brightness
Bausch & Lomb				
8x42 WP Elite	full-size	29	5	28
10x42 WP Elite	full-size	28	5	18
7x26 Custom	compact	13	6	14
10x42 WP Discoverer	full-size	30	8	18
8x24 Legacy	compact	8	8	9
Brunton				
7.5x43 Epoch	full-size	25	3	28
10.5x43 Epoch	full-size	25	3	18
7x42 Eterna	full-size	34	5.5	28
10x42 Eterna	full-size	34	6	18
Bushnell				
8x42 Legend	full-size	30	6	28
10x42 Legend	full-size	30	6	18

Brand	size	weight (in oz.)	closest focus	brightness
Eagle				
8x42 Ranger PC	full-size	23	5.2	28
10x42 Ranger PC	full-size	23	5.2	18
6x32 Ranger Platinum	full-size	19	3	28
8x32 Ranger Platinum	full-size	19	3	14
Kahles				
8x42 DCF	full-size	26	8	28
10x42 DCF	full-size	26	8	18
8x32 DCF	full-size	22	5	14
Leica				
8x32 BN Ultra	full-size	22	7	16
10x32 Trinovid Ultra	full-size	24	7	10
Minox				
8x32 BD/BR	full-size	22	5	16
10x42 BD/BR	full-size	27	8	16
Nikon				
8x20 Venturer LX	compact	10	8	9
8x32 Venturer LX	full-size	25	8	16
8x42 Venturer LX	full-size	35	9	28
8x42 Monarch ATB/PC	full-size	21	8	28
Pentax				
8x32 DCF WP	full-size	23	7	16
8x42 DCF WP	full-size	27	8	28
10x42 DCF WP	full-size	27	9	18
10x24 UCF MC	compact	12	7	6
Swarovski				
8x20 B/G	compact	8	8	6
8.5x42 EL	full-size	29	8	24
10x42 EL	full-size	28	8	18
Swift				
7x36 Eaglet WP	full-size	21	5	26
10x42 Viceroy WP	full-size	24	6	18
8x25 Trilyte	compact	14	8	9
10x25 Trilyte	compact	14	8	6
Zeiss				
10x40 Victory	full-size	26	8	16

Index

A

Aeshnidae 22
Canada Darner 26
Aeshna canadensis 26
Aeshna clepsydra 38
Aeshna constricta 36
Aeshna eremita 30
Aeshna interrupta 40
Aeshna juncea 39
Aeshna sitchensis 44
Aeshna subarctica 42
Aeshna tuberculifera 32
Aeshna umbrosa 34
Aeshna verticalis 28
American Emerald 106
Anax junius 46
Arigomphus cornutus 80
Arigomphus furcifer 81
Arrow Clubtail 74
Arrowhead Spiketail 94
Ashy Clubtail 64

B

Band-winged Meadowhawk 152
Basiaeschna janata 55
Baskettail
—Beaverpond 114
—Common 110
—Prince 115
—Spiny 112
Baskettails 110
Beaverpond Baskettail 114
Black Meadowhawk 150
Black Saddlebags 184
Black-shouldered Spinyleg 78
Black-tipped Darner 32
Blue Dasher 166
Boghaunter, Ebony 109
Boreal Snaketail 84
Boyeria grafiana 48
Boyeria vinosa 50
Brown Spiketail 98
Brush-tipped Emerald 116

C

Calico Pennant 182
Canada Whiteface 174
Carolina Saddlebags 192
Celithemis elisa 182

Celithemis eponina 183
Chalk-fronted Corporal 148
Cherry-faced Meadowhawk 153
Clamp-tipped Emerald 118
Clubtail
—Arrow 74
—Ashy 64
—Cobra 69
—Dusky 62
—Elusive 75
—Green-faced 60
—Horned 80
—Lancet 65
—Least 82
—Lilypad 81
—Midland 72
—Mustached 61
—Pronghorn 68
—Rapids 66
—Riverine 76
—Skillet 70
—Splendid 73
—Zebra 77
Clubtails 56
Cobra Clubtail 69
Common Baskettail 110
Common Green Darner 46
Common Sanddragon 83
Common Whitetail 144
Cordulegaster bilineata 98
Cordulegaster diastatops 96
Cordulegaster maculata 93
Cordulegaster obliqua 94
Cordulegasteridae 92
Cordulia shurtleffii 106
Corduliidae 104
Corporal, Chalk-fronted 148
Crimson-ringed Whiteface 176
Cruiser
—Illinois River Cruiser 102
—Stream Cruiser 100
Cruisers 99
Cyrano Darner 52

D

Darner
—Black-tipped 32
—Canada 26
—Common Green 46
—Cyrano 52
—Fawn 50
—Green 46

—Green-striped 28
—Harlequin 53
—Lake 30
—Lance-tipped 36
—Mottled 38
—Ocellated 48
—Sedge 39
—Shadow 34
—Springtime 55
—Subarctic 42
—Swamp 54
—Variable 40
—Zigzag 44
Darners 22
Dasher, Blue 166
Delicate Emerald 120
Delta-spotted Spiketail 96
Didymops transversa 100
Dorocordulia libera 108
Dot-tailed Whiteface 172
Dragonhunter 58
Dromogomphus spinosus 78
Dusky Clubtail 62

E

Eastern Pondhawk 168
Ebony Boghaunter 109
Elfin Skimmer 164
Elusive Clubtail 75
Emerald
—American 106
—Brush-tipped 116
—Clamp-tipped 118
—Delicate 120
—Forcipate 121
—Hine's 122
—Hudsonian 123
—Incurvate 124
—Kennedy's 125
—Lake 126
—Ocellated 127
—Plains 128
—Racket-tailed 108
—Ringed 129
—Ski-tailed 130
—Williamson's 132
Emeralds 104
Epiaeschna heros 54
Epicordulia princeps 115
Epitheca canis 114
Epitheca cynosura 110
Epitheca princeps 115

Epitheca spinigera 112
Erythemis simplicicollis 168
Extra-striped Snaketail 86

F

Fawn Darner 50
Forcipate Emerald 121
Four-spotted Skimmer 138
Frosted Whiteface 180

G

Glider
—Spot-winged 170
—Wandering 171
Gomphaeschna furcillata 53
Gomphidae 56
Gomphus adelphus 61
Gomphus exilis 65
Gomphus fraternus 72
Gomphus graslinellus 68
Gomphus lineatifrons 73
Gomphus lividus 64
Gomphus quadricolor 66
Gomphus spicatus 62
Gomphus vastus 69
Gomphus ventricosus 70
Gomphus viridifrons 60
Green-faced Clubtail 60
Green-striped Darner 28

H

Hagenius brevistylus 58
Halloween Pennant 183
Harlequin Darner 53
Hine's Emerald 122
Horned Clubtail 80
Hudsonian Emerald 123
Hudsonian Whiteface 175

IJK

Illinois River Cruiser 102
Incurvate Emerald 124
Kennedy's Emerald 125

L

Ladona julia 148
Lake Darner 30
Lake Emerald 126
Lance-tipped Darner 36
Lancet Clubtail 65
Least Clubtail 82
Leucorrhinia frigida 180
Leucorrhinia glacialis 176
Leucorrhinia hudsonica 175

Leucorrhinia intacta 172
Leucorrhinia patricia 174
Leucorrhinia proxima 178
Libellula julia 148
Libellula incesta 140
Libellula luctuosa 146
Libellula pulchella 142
Libellula quadrimaculata 138
Libellula lydia 144
Libellulidae 136
Lilypad Clubtail 81

M
Macromia illinoiensis 102
Macromiidae 99
Meadowhawk
—Band-winged 152
—Black 150
—Cherry-faced 153
—Ruby 154
—Saffron-winged 156
—Variegated 162
—White-faced 158
—Yellow-legged 160
Meadowhawks 136
Midland Clubtail 72
Mottled Darner 38
Mustached Clubtail 61

N
Nannothemis bella 164
Nasiaeschna pentacantha 52
Neurocordulia yamaskanensis 134

O
Ocellated Darner 48
Ocellated Emerald 127
Ophiogomphus anomalus 86
Ophiogomphus carolus 88
Ophiogomphus colubrinus 84
Ophiogomphus howei 87
Ophiogomphus rupinsulensis 89
Ophiogomphus species 91
Ophiogomphus susbehcha 90

P
Pachydiplax longipennis 166
Pantala flavescens 171
Pantala hymenaea 170
Pennant
—Calico 182
—Halloween 183
Plains Emerald 128

Plathemis lydia 144
Pondhawk, Eastern 168
Prince Baskettail 115
Progomphus obscurus 83
Pronghorn Clubtail 68
Pygmy Snaketail 87

R
Racket-tailed Emerald 108
Rapids Clubtail 66
Red Saddlebags 192
Red-waisted Whiteface 178
Riffle Snaketail 88
Ringed Emerald 129
Riverine Clubtail 76
Ruby Meadowhawk 154
Rusty Snaketail 89

S
Saddlebags, Black 184
Saffron-winged Meadowhawk 156
Sand Snaketail 91
Sanddragon, Common 83
Sedge Darner 39
Shadow Darner 34
Shadowdragon, Stygian 134
Ski-tailed Emerald 130
Skillet Clubtail 70
Skimmer
—Elfin 164
—Four-spotted 138
—Slaty 140
—Twelve-spotted 142
—Widow 146
Skimmers 136
Slaty Skimmer 140
Snaketail
—Boreal 84
—Extra-striped 86
—Pygmy 87
—Riffle 88
—Rusty 89
—Sand 91
—Wisconsin 90
Somatochlora albicincta 129
Somatochlora cingulata 126
Somatochlora elongata 130
Somatochlora ensigera 128
Somatochlora forcipata 121
Somatochlora franklini 120
Somatochlora hineana 122
Somatochlora hudsonica 123

Somatochlora incurvata 124
Somatochlora kennedyi 125
Somatochlora minor 127
Somatochlora tenebrosa 118
Somatochlora walshii 116
Somatochlora williamsoni 132
Spiketail
—Arrowhead 94
—Brown 98
—Delta-spotted 96
—Twin-spotted 93
Spiketails 92
Spiny Baskettail 112
Spinyleg, Black-shouldered 78
Splendid Clubtail 73
Spot-winged Glider 170
Springtime Darner 55
Stream Cruiser 100
Stygian Shadowdragon 134
Stylogomphus albistylus 82
Stylurus amnicola 76
Stylurus notatus 75
Stylurus scudderi 77
Stylurus spiniceps 74
Subarctic Darner 42
Swamp Darner 54
Sympetrum corruptum 162
Sympetrum costiferum 156
Sympetrum danae 150
Sympetrum internum 153
Sympetrum obtrusum 158
Sympetrum rubicundulum 154
Sympetrum semicinctum 152
Sympetrum vicinum 160

T

Tetragoneuria canis 114
Tetragoneuria cynosura 110
Tetragoneuria spinigera 112
Tramea carolina 192
Tramea lacerata 184
Tramea onusta 192
Twelve-spotted Skimmer 142
Twin-spotted Spiketail 93

UVW

Variable Darner 40
Variegated Meadowhawk 162
Wandering Glider 171
White-faced Meadowhawk 158
Whiteface
—Canada 174

—Crimson-ringed 176
—Dot-tailed 172
—Frosted 180
—Hudsonian 175
—Red-waisted 178
Whitefaces 136
Widow Skimmer 146
Williamson's Emerald 132
Williamsonia fletcheri 109
Wisconsin Snaketail 90

XYZ

Yellow-legged Meadowhawk 160
Zebra Clubtail 77
Zigzag Darner 44

Field Notes

Field Notes

Field Notes

Field Notes